PERSONAL
DEVELOPMENT
WITH THE
TAROT

*This book is dedicated to the
generations before us and to come after us.*

*For Joe, Sally, Lisa and Seth.
In the hope of peace for Jasmine and her children.*

PERSONAL DEVELOPMENT
WITH THE
TAROT

CATHERINE SUMMERS
AND JULIAN VAYNE

quantum

LONDON • NEW YORK • TORONTO • SYDNEY

quantum

An imprint of W. Foulsham & Co. Ltd
The Publishing House, Bennetts Close,
Cippenham, Slough, Berkshire SL1 5AP, England

ISBN 0–572–02462-2

Previously published as *Self Development with the Tarot*.

Printed in Great Britain by St Edmundsbury Press, Bury St Edmunds, Suffolk

Contents

Introduction

ver the course of human history there have been periodic shifts in the patterns of human society. The distant beginnings of human history are a mystery to us; however, according to esoteric theory the evolution of human consciousness takes place in a series of periods known as aeons. The last two thousand years is referred to as the Aeon of Osiris, a time in which God has been regarded as male, and his word communicated through an almost exclusively male series of gurus and prophets. The previous aeon, the Aeon of Isis, was dominated by the figure of the goddess, with female-centred cults flourishing around the ancient world.

Today we are emerging into the dawn of a new aeon, a new shift in the development of human society and consciousness. This era goes by many different names, such as the Aeon of Horus, the Age of Aquarius, or the New Age.

We must not make the mistake of assuming that the New Age will be from the start a Golden Age. At present we can see the delicate and often difficult transition might be likened to a time of personal crisis. The individual may be troubled, thrown into confusion; yet in the midst of his or her trials the opportunity to reassess the past and to emerge into a new future presents itself.

There are drastic changes in every aspect of our society. Information technology has spread a vast web of communication systems across the globe; the ills of pollution and social degradation from industrialisation are rife. As these changes occur at both a national and a global level, so they are mirrored in the life of the individual. Changing social morals and scientific developments pose questions for each of us as much as they do for governments. People are becoming increasingly aware of the importance of personal development, of discovering themselves and their place in our rapidly changing world.

The New Age outlook puts an emphasis on a holistic, relationship-centred approach. Just as western industrialised society has had to review the relationship between humanity and nature (moving from a view of exploitation to symbiosis), so a new view is emerging of the relationship between the individual and the secret workings of the mind.

Two important features have emerged during the dawn of this New Age. The first is that, as access to historical and contemporary information increases, we are no longer constrained to see the universe through one ethnic ideal or philosophy. Today we have access to the folk legends of the Hopi Indians as easily as to the latest philosophical paradigms of sub-atomic physics. To paraphrase the mythographer Joseph Campbell, by comparative mythology our understanding of our roles as individuals and our relationship to 'God' has been liberated from the limited perspective of a solely cultural context.

The second major feature of New Age thought is related to self-responsibility. Applied psychological techniques (co-counselling, hypnotherapy and many more) are increasingly being used to improve individual performance and abilities. In business, psychological techniques to promote self-awareness are used to extend the skills of individuals and to strengthen areas in which they are less able (assertiveness training and interpersonal communication courses are two of the most widely used).

This combination of an eclectic attitude to religious or philosophical systems is being coupled with the attitude that the individual is, ultimately, self-responsible. The New Age ethos is that understanding develops by personal effort, not through the intercession of a particular credo or teacher. We have innumerable methods available to discover our inner selves but the impetus to do so is in the hands of the individual.

Many people, often as the result of a life crisis or through a gradually increasing interest, feel a pressing need to get in touch with themselves and to discover, in their own unique way, their own nature and place in the universe. In the search for a method that may be used for personal development, they are turning to sources of inspiration from ancient times, sources that predate or transcend any particular cultural or religious ethos. One such system is the tarot.

Psychology and the Tarot

Throughout this book we have drawn on the work of Carl Gustav Jung (1875–1961) as the psychological foundation from which the tarot may be understood. Unlike the rigid behaviourist school, Jung and his followers saw the human psyche as a rich tapestry of forces and interactions. Jung's work used art therapy to access aspects of the human personality that did not have a directly conscious expression. Through his work with dream analysis, Jung began to notice the recurrence of particular symbols in the dreams of many individuals. This led him to examine ancient systems of symbolism – the I Ching, alchemy, astrology, the tarot, and many more. Jung realised that mystical or magical thought was the psychology of the past and that it was just as valid to the present.

Increasingly, modern psychologists are discovering for themselves the validity of ancient symbolic systems. Using psychological terminology is advantageous in giving a contemporary understanding of the tarot deck, free of arcane esoteric language. Psychological terms increase the accessibility of the tarot as well as providing a view that is not confused by occult terms or restricted to a single religious credo.

The Origins of the Cards

There is evidence that playing cards existed from the beginning of the fourteenth century and that a rudimentary tarot was present by the fifteenth century. It is certain that the main picture cards, the skeleton of the tarot, were established by the sixteenth century.

Perhaps the most popular theory is that the tarot represents a distillation of esoteric wisdom from ancient Egypt. Indeed, the deck is often referred to as the 'Book of Thoth' after the Egyptian god of writing and magic.

Some writers trace the origin of the cards to the symbolism of the Hindu god Vishnu. Vishnu was the preserving aspect of the triad

Hindu deity. He is often depicted holding four objects – a lotus, a mace, a conch shell and a discus – which may have been the precursors of the four tarot suits. Vishnu's ten traditional avatars also parallel the ten sephiroth of the Hebrew Tree of Life, from which western Qabalists believed the tarot to derive.

Before the Spanish invasion of South America, the Aztecs had a number of hand-painted codices that scholars claim bear some relation to the picture cards of the tarot.

There are widely conflicting views on the origin of the cards; some claim they were carried by migrating peoples from India (the forebears of the modern gypsies). Although the arrival of the cards in Europe (assuming they did not have an indigenous origin there) predates the gypsies, it may be that they popularised the deck through its divinatory use. Most of the documentation from the medieval period comprises secular and religious texts outlawing the use of cards for gaming and gambling.

The amalgamation of the two sets of cards, the Minor and Major Arcanas, into one deck may have been the work of an eleventh-century heretical Christian sect called the Waldenses. They travelled Europe in search of converts and may have used the cards as a means of teaching through allegorical symbolism and story.

The tarot deck continued to be used to play the excruciatingly complex game of Tarocchi, surfacing in various guises. Certainly the cards have formed the spiritual focus for generations of mystics, scholars and occultists. As a tool for prediction, the tarot has found favour with kings, popes, generals and lovers for hundreds of years.

During the nineteenth century there was a resurgence in the use of the tarot as a tool for personal development. The impetus for this revival came primarily from an esoteric group called the Order of the Golden Dawn, which flourished in Britain. The Golden Dawn, the Theosophical Society, the Rosicrucians and others saw the tarot not as a lowly deck of game cards but as a series of images representing the total knowledge of the entire world. The sires of these groups rediscovered the rich strata of symbolism that slept beneath the surface of each card. They re-energised the cards by creating the new decks that form the basis of most modern renderings of the cards.

The eclectic interest in philosophies and attitudes to human nature that grew in the 1960s and 1970s resulted in a continued interest in the tarot and the exploration of the many ways in which it could be used. In the last 20 years many reprints of older decks, as well as new variations, have become generally available. Tarot packs today have a wide range of visual styles, from those that focus on a particular mythology (such as the Arthurian cycle) to those that strive for a highly contemporary interpretation of the images.

The obscure history of the tarot aside, today we are presented with a range of artistic interpretations, all holding the same core symbolism. The tarot provides a valuable and consistent method of personal development and is therefore of tremendous value.

The Form of the Tarot

The tarot deck consists of 78 cards that fall into many divisions and sub-divisions. The primary division in the deck is into the Major Arcana and Minor Arcana cards (the word Arcana may be taken to mean 'book'). The Major Arcana, or trump cards, are 22 in number. The remaining 56 cards comprise four suits, in much the same way as playing cards. The Minor Arcana suits range from ace to ten (the 'pip' cards) plus four 'court' cards.

The names given to the cards vary from deck to deck; however the basis of the tarot is as follows:

The Major Arcana

Numeral	Title	Alternative title(s)
0	The Fool	
I	The Magus	The Magician, The High Priest
II	The Priestess	The High Priestess, The Papess
III	The Empress	
IV	The Emperor	
V	The Hierophant	The Pope
VI	The Lovers	The Brothers
VII	The Chariot	
VIII	Adjustment	Justice (can be numbered XI)
IX	The Hermit	

X	Fortune	The Wheel of Fortune
XI	Lust	Strength (can be numbered VIII)
XII	The Hanged Man	
XIII	Death	
XIV	Art	Temperance
XV	The Devil	The Horned One
XVI	The Tower	War, The House of God
XVII	The Star	
XVIII	The Moon	
XIX	The Sun	
XX	The Aeon	Judgement
XXI	The World	The Universe

Tarot decks that conform to a particular mythology often use titles drawn from the myth they utilise. However, the fundamental pattern is usually quite clear. Thus, in the Egyptian tarot, card XII is called 'Sacrifice' but in all other respects is clearly the Hanged Man.

The same diversity of nomenclature is to be found in the Minor Arcana, both with the names given to the four suits and to the court cards in each suit. Some of the commonest variations are:

Suit Name	Alternatives
Wands	Batons, Sceptres, Clubs
Cups	Goblets, Chalices, Vessels
Swords	Spears, Blades, Knives
Discs	Coins, Pentacles, Shields

The court cards follow the suit names. Thus in the Thoth deck we find the Knight, Queen, Prince and Princess for each of the four suits of Wands, Cups, Swords and Discs. However, in other decks the court card names may differ:

Court Card	Alternatives
Knight	King, Patriarch
Queen	Matriarch
Prince	Knight, Warrior
Princess	Maiden, Page

In order to use the tarot as a tool for personal development you will need to obtain your own deck. This book has been written in such a way that its use is not dependent on any particular pack. Your choice of tarot deck should be guided by your own intuition and aesthetic sense – it would be fruitless to obtain a deck that is highly recommended for meditational purposes if you dislike the artistic style. The vital factor is that the images of the cards should be ones with which you can identify and which inspire you. It is best to avoid cards with 'cartoon style' images, which tend towards superficiality. Cards with too much ornate design or text also tend to distract the mind from the essential symbolism. Go to a shop that stocks a wide range of cards and look through the packs until you find one you feel at home with. As a guide you may like to look at the following decks:

- The Golden Dawn – *good clear colours*
- The Sacred Rose – *colourful, symbolic images based on medieval stained glass*
- The Winged Spirit Tarot – *images of winged spirit messengers bridging the gap between humans and angels*
- The Thoth Tarot – *a profound and well-painted rendering (the large-sized deck may be helpful for contemplation)*

Many modern decks are visually orientated around a particular mythology. Current packs include those with North American Indian, Egyptian and, increasingly, Celtic and native European symbolism. Other decks approach the tarot through a specific metaphor, such as the feminist-orientated Motherpeace tarot.

The advantages of such packs are that they may attract you by virtue of stimulating a particular affinity with a given culture or mythos. The disadvantage is that a deck that is too bound into one set of symbols may limit the messages the cards will give you. Celtic symbolism, for instance, is a fine spark for some people but it would be a mistake to see the world through exclusively Celtic-coloured spectacles.

Figure 1: Examples from different tarot decks

Deck: Golden Dawn
Card: The Hierophant

Deck: Sacred Rose
Card: The Moon

Deck: Winged Spirit
Card: Justice

Deck: Thoth
Card: The Emperor

Once you have a deck that you are content to use, get to know it! Look through the cards and acquaint yourself with each one. Don't worry about learning any symbolism or memorising the contents of any booklet that came with the deck. You may want to keep your cards wrapped in a length of fabric (traditionally black silk) and in a private place when not using them. For the purposes of personal development you will need to give yourself and your cards the opportunity to get to know each other, so look at and handle your deck often.

Along with your tarot it is advisable to buy a book to use as a diary or notebook. In this you will be able to record the results arrived at through your study of the cards. You may also wish to keep a record of your dreams as these can provide a useful window into your unconscious state.

———Chapter 1———
The Nature of the Tarot

arot cards do not have an intrinsic power; their only power comes from their use, and that use does not necessitate conforming to any particular belief system. As the terms 'Arcana' and 'Book of Thoth' suggest, the cards are a repository of hidden knowledge. That knowledge is revealed from the way in which they relate to you. Each image in the deck is part of a pictorial library designed to correspond to the many levels and experiences of the individual. The symbolism of the deck is a model of the human psyche, with varied aspects of meaning, interpretation and application. Each card may be perceived as being a window into the mind of the individual. The visual nature of the tarot provides an immediate series of images that reflect one's own inner nature. In developing a relationship with each of the cards, the individual actually develops a deeper understanding of the self.

Jung and the Tarot

Using the terminology of Jungian psychology, the tarot is a series of *archetypal forces* described in visual form. Jung used the term 'archetypal' to mean an unconscious force that exists and acts independently of the human consciousness. His theory, however, was a modern expression of an ancient idea. In different cultures, religions and individuals, the conscious expression of an archetype will vary. However, there is an identical core to be found in all variations on the archetypal motif. Thus the archetype of the 'dying god' appears in Christian imagery as Christ crucified, in Norse myth as Odin slain, and in the tarot as the Hanged Man. The process of personal development (which Jung called *individuation*) entails the developing of a communication between the conscious mind and these archetypal forces. By exploring, experiencing, understanding and integrating the archtypes of the unconscious, the central work of personal development – to 'know thyself' – may be embarked upon.

By identifying the archetypal forces that form the basis of your consciousness, you will recognise, through experience, how these forces affect you and those about you. As you discover that each card is a mirror of yourself, you will be able to use these aspects of your own nature to their fullest potential.

The archetypal forces that Jung identified in the human psyche are: the Great Mother; the Father God; the Guide; the Shadow; and the Animus/Anima. Within the tarot system all these archetypal forces (and, arguably, a number of others that Jung did not identify) appear in many different guises.

The Great Mother

This archetypal force represents the female forces of the universe, both the external world and the internal psychic realm. This archetype represents the nature of woman, in all her aspects. Although referred to as 'Mother', this archetype may show the aspect of woman as maiden, mother, whore or grandmother, depending on the facet that is exposed. Thus in the tarot deck one might say that the High Priestess is the maiden aspect; the Empress is the mother; Strength is the whore; and the Moon is the grandmother or hag. 'Whore' in this context refers to the phase in the life of a woman when she is sexually mature but need not focus her sexuality in reproductive terms. The word 'whore' originally had moral and social connotations far different from those of the present day – the priestesses of certain ancient temples were known as 'sacred whores' because they were not partnered to any single aspect of the god force. Each different facet of this archetype shows the female force in either active or passive mode (for more information on this archetype see our book *Seeds of Magick*, see page 155).

The Father God

Again this figure appears in a multitude of ways in myth, folklore and in the tarot. While the Goddess archetype has four main aspects, the God archetype has only two: he is either the dark, wintry lord of the underworld (the Devil or Death) or the bright, summery lord of the fertile overworld (the Emperor or the Hierophant). As with the Great Mother archetype, these are complementary facets of the same system.

The Guide

Within the tarot, the Guide appears as a figure that helps the individual through the tangled, hidden byways of the unconscious mind. The most common feature of this archetype is his mercurial nature. Frequently he is shown as a bisexual or epicene figure whose role it is to mediate between different layers of experience and existence. In the tarot deck, the Magician, Temperance and the Hermit could be associated with this archetype.

The Shadow

This figure is more closely associated with the working of the persona than with an intrinsic element in the unconscious. The Shadow is a confused figure in that it represents those aspects of the psyche which act 'negatively' (meaning, in this case, detrimentally) when a particular aspect of the self has been ignored or repressed. In one sense, the Shadow acts as an arbiter or prompt from the unconscious level that makes itself felt in the conscious mind. This may be seen in the changes of mental state that cards such as the Hanged Man or Judgement symbolise.

The Animus/Anima

The Animus is the masculine force found in the female psyche, while the Anima is the archetype of feminine force found in the male unconscious.

The tarot deviates from Jung's understanding of these terms. He saw the Anima as existing in the man and the Animus in the woman. As these forces are concerned with quality (masculine and feminine) and not gender (male or female), each individual carries both sets of qualities irrespective of their physical gender. In the tarot, the marriage of unconscious feminine and masculine traits is shown as being necessary in the individual of whichever sex. Cards that demonstrate this marriage of opposites might be the Lovers or Temperance.

In all the examples given above the archetypal forces are not limited to one card only. For instance, the card Temperance shows the marriage of Animus/Anima, but the figure presiding over the alchemical marriage could also be considered as being an aspect of the Great Mother archetype. As whole images, all cards in the deck show different archetypes, in particular aspects, in any given image.

The Persona and the Ego

The persona is not an archetypal force, rather it is the social mechanism through which the unconscious manifests. The word 'persona' means mask, the face the individual presents to the world which, though broadly constant, will vary under different circumstances. Thus Mrs X may have certain traits in her personality that tend to remain constant, though different aspects of it will be displayed when she is working in the office, at home with her children or in the arms of her partner. An important feature of the persona is that it is as much a self-image (i.e. an image that is projected on to the conscious mind) as it is an image projected outward when dealing with others.

At certain times different forces within the unconscious will dominate or alter the persona; for instance the Mother archetype may become the dominant force within the persona when a woman is pregnant. The danger with this is that the persona can become static and, usually by a combination of internal and external factors, our hypothetical woman will become trapped in her sole role as mother.

The ego (the consciously recognised and identified features of the persona) is a much maligned term. We speak of 'egocentric' or 'egotistic' people and tend to forget the positive features of this part of the psyche. The major feature of the ego is that it maintains the sense of self-identity, the psychic integrity of the individual as being separate and distinct from other non-self features of the universe. It is the ego that allows the mind to distinguish self from other people, objects and events. When damage to the ego level occurs, the individual may find it impossible to distinguish between events in the self (such as emotions) and outside influences; a sense of paranoia or of intolerable responsibility for everything (guilt) is the most common result.

In personal development, the ego and the persona as a whole are turned from rigid units to fluid structures. Rather than being panes of dirty glass that obscure the interaction between conscious and unconscious minds, they become lenses that can be used to focus, increase or depress these channels of integral communication as the situation dictates.

The Unconscious and Conscious Minds

The human psyche mirrors the outside world. This idea goes by many names but is best known as the microcosm/macrocosm theory. That is, what exists within the self is mirrored by or reflects what exists outside the self.

In trying to comprehend the different levels of one's own being, the simplest model is the triple mind diagram (see Fig. 2). This shows that the role of the ego is to mediate between the conscious, rational and linear area and the unconscious, irrational and conceptual area. The

Figure 2: The triple mind

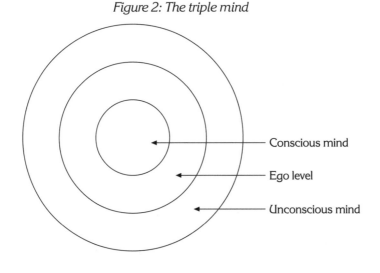

Conscious mind

Ego level

Unconscious mind

greatest difficulty with understanding the term 'unconscious' is the universality of this level. To appreciate the way in which the unconscious works, arbitrary divisions may be made within it to explain how this level of the self is at once highly personal and also collective.

The analyst Sigmund Freud (1856–1939) viewed the unconscious or subconscious mind as a sort of garbage heap to which the remnants of complexes, repressed memories and desires were relegated. Jung's view and the modern extension of his theories have a quite different perspective. Certainly the unconscious in psychology has marked similarities to a number of collective 'spirits' or psychic states spoken of in ancient cultures.

In examining the unconscious, a series of levels can be used to give an idea about the nature of this system – for, by definition, the conscious mind cannot comprehend, much less know, the unconscious mind in totality (see Fig. 3). The personal unconscious is the storehouse of individual memories, associations and concepts. The group unconscious contains imagery that relates to one's own social, religious or ethnic background. The collective unconscious contains instincts, patterns and images common to all human beings.

For example, the female instinct to defend her offspring is inherent in the human unconscious; it is biologically programmed at the

Figure 3: Levels of the unconscious mind

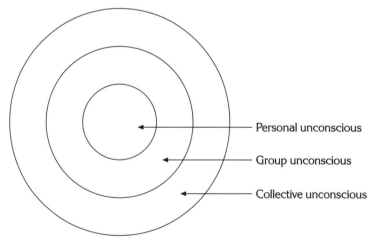

deepest, most basic level. The ancient Egyptians personified this force as the goddess Sekhmet, who represented the protective, defensive and aggressive features of the psyche. This image and also images from other cultures exist at the group unconscious level. In terms of the group unconscious, there are differing social, moral and ancestral factors that may modify the defensive reaction. At the personal level of the unconscious, the individual will have certain associations, ideas or memories that relate to personal experiences of this biological programme in action.

Words and pictures

In exploring the relationship between the unconscious and conscious minds, a common language that both levels can comprehend is necessary. Naturally a common language is vital for communication; it is for just such a reason that scientists adopted the use of Latin terminology in their work, so that *Felis domesticus* is understood even if in his or her native tongue the biologist would commonly name the creature 'cat'.

The difference, in mental terms, is that the unconscious mind communicates in images and emotions, whereas the conscious mind communicates in letters, numbers and words. The tarot combines both these features, each card having rational, logical associations and also unconscious, symbolic associations. It is for just this reason that the tarot is such an excellent tool for personal development – it can be appreciated, understood and processed by all levels of being.

When learning about the tarot, the key is to develop both areas – rational and emotional. By appreciating the tarot intellectually and also intuitively it provides a window through which information can be exchanged, mutually, through all areas of the mind.

Meaningful Chance

The tarot is best known as a method of divination or (less politely or accurately) fortune-telling. Again, this predictive feature of the cards has parallels within the work of Jung.

Jung outlined a theory known as synchronicity or the theory of meaningful chance. He observed that there seemed to be a connecting principle between occurrences, irrespective of whether one directly caused the other (hence the term 'acausal'). The vital feature of synchronistic theory is that apparently chaotic or chance events can convey meaning to the person(s) concerned. To quote from Bill Anderton's *Life Cycles,* 'a stranger passes me in the street, a chance event; a person I have not seen in ten years passes me in the street – a meaningful chance event'.

In the apparently random (that is, random from the perspective of the conscious mind) fall of a series of tarot cards, there lies the possibility of learning to discern the meaningful pattern that results. Naturally the ego may project any number of pure fantasies or delusions on the interpretation of the spread. However, by developing a simultaneously objective and intuitive approach, a genuine interpretation will evolve.

In the context of personal development, the divinatory function of the tarot need not be at the fore. However, an appreciation of the synchronistic patterns in life and an understanding of the holistic intertwining of individual events are required.

As you use the tarot for personal development purposes you may begin to notice an increase in the number of synchronistic events in your life. One might be studying the Magician card and, the next morning, see a television programme about clowns (a figure often representing the trickster aspect of the Magician), and this could be followed up in any number of meaningful ways, i.e. by events, symbols or experiences that somehow remind you of the card in question. Such meaningful chances are not to be found by obsessive behaviour, or to be forced by the over-zealous conscious mind, desperately seeking to see connections where there really are none. Synchronistic events are messages, projected on to outer reality, from the unconscious. Thus they may act as signposts, either suggesting that you are pursuing the correct course or advising you to look in other directions for the answers you seek.

The Cycle of the Tarot

Everything in the universe is cyclical; therefore the tarot, being a mirror of the universe, is also cyclical. In nature, night follows day, spring follows winter, and in the tarot each card represents a point on an ever-turning wheel of change. The very word 'tarot' is an example of this cyclic flow. As MacGregor Mathers (one of the founding members of the Golden Dawn) points out, the word tarot can be seen as an anagram of other words. The final 't' in tarot (which is not pronounced) reaffirms the cyclic pattern. In Hebrew we find the word 'rota', which means a wheel, and the word 'tora', which means a holy book.

In the visual symbolism of the deck, the Fool card has the same function as the letter 't' in the word tarot. The Fool is number zero and in different decks is placed either at the beginning or at the end of the 78-card run. Thus this card is both the beginning and the ending, alpha and omega. The number zero is also a circle, and in the visual symbolism of many decks the Fool is shown carrying a knapsack filled with coins or discs. This connects the Fool as the 'first' card to the 'last' card, the Ten of Discs. The allegorical meaning of this symbolism is that the Fool, as the representative of the individual, carries with him all that he needs for his journey through the archetypal levels of experience. In the same way it is not the tarot cards themselves that will help you in your own development – they are only 78 painted cards. Rather it is by using the tarot as a tool to unlock the different areas of your inner nature that you will find wisdom. Archetypal powers are not 'out there' but inside you. The challenge is to realise this.

The Major Arcana of the tarot are representations of the central archetypal forces. The images of the Mother and Father forces, the Hero and the Guide, are inherent in them, as are figures that symbolise the major transforming events in human life: birth, love, death, rebirth.

In the Minor Arcana there is an important sub-division into the four suits. Each suit corresponds to an Element:

Suit	Element	
Wands	Fire	
Cups	Water	*(In some decks Wands are associated with*
Swords	Air	*Air and Swords with Fire)*
Discs	Earth	

The Elements are terms used to describe a number of features of the universe. In the context of personal development they describe aspects of the psyche. Each elemental term is in fact a shorthand way of expressing a complex web of associated ideas:

- Fire: *strength, will-power, violence, passion, creativity*
- Water: *passivity, emotion, sensitivity, intuition, indolence*
- Air: *intelligence, flexibility, wit, swiftness, unreliability*
- Earth: *stability, fertility, materialism, caution, loyalty*

Figure 4: The Arcana of the tarot and the Elements

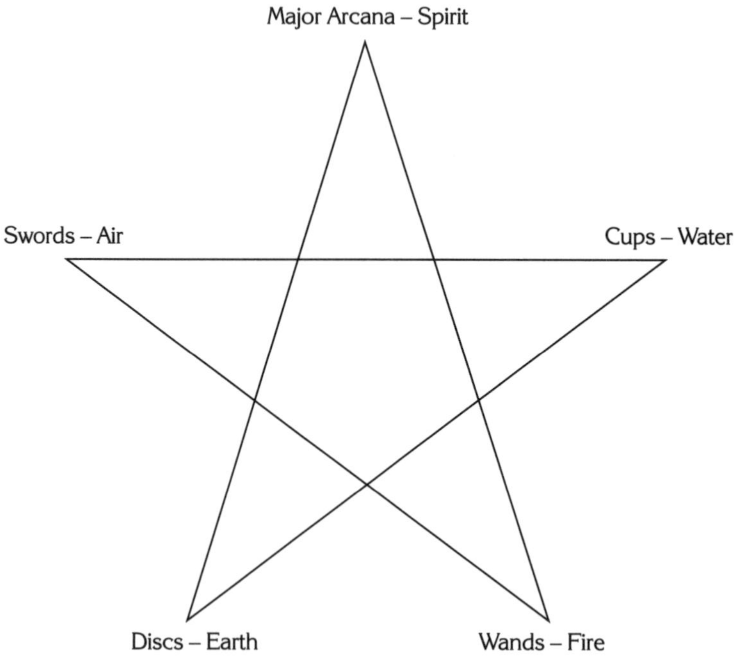

Major Arcana – Spirit

Swords – Air

Cups – Water

Discs – Earth

Wands – Fire

As you can see from the list above, though each Element has a range of associations, there is a common thread throughout. In the visual language of the tarot the Elements appear in many ways. For instance, the suit of Cups is obviously linked to the Element of Water. Often specific colours are used to give another visual dimension to the Elemental attributes. Fire is accorded reds and golds, while earthy qualities and ideas are associated with colours such as green and brown. Air cards may be coloured sky blue or pale yellow and water cards in sea greens and deep blues.

The elemental system provides another way of looking at your own nature. For instance, your personal drive (Fire) is applied through your intellect (Air) and supported by your intuition (Water) and manifests through your physical body (Earth).

In describing the Elements, Fire and Air are said to be 'masculine-positive' while Water and Earth are 'feminine-negative'. The psyche of each individual has both negative and positive traits. These are complementary or polar aspects, just as summer and winter are complementary sides of the same cycle. Negative aspects, such as passivity and stability, are as necessary to form an integrated and whole psyche as positive ones, such as aggression and intellect. It is important to remember that the terms masculine and feminine refer to qualities, as do the symbolic genders shown in the symbolism of the tarot. Human beings, irrespective of their physical gender, should aim to cultivate a harmonious range of abilities, and the use of male and female images in the deck recall this to mind. For example, the Empress may represent the caring, protective and sustaining aspects in the human nature but her archetypal message is as relevant to the physical male as it is to the female.

Chapter 2

The Tarot as a Tool of Personal Development

ny method of personal development relies on the development of two skills: relaxation and concentration. These abilities are often seen as opposites whereas they are actually complementary. For example, a golfer must learn how to relax his or her muscles and banish performance anxiety but must also be able to concentrate on the shot above everything else, holding a clear and steady purpose in mind as the strike is aimed. To relax the mind and body frees the consciousness so that a given subject (in this case one or more tarot images) may be concentrated upon.

The relaxation process must begin with your choice of time and place. For all of the practices we give below you will need to find a time when you will not be disturbed and a place that is, as far as possible, comfortable and free from distractions. To assist in relaxing your body loose-fitting clothing and moderate lighting (candlelight relaxes the eyes and aids concentration) are best. The use of 'ambient music' is unlikely to be of value, having more of a disruptive effect than a relaxing one. A light incense (joss sticks will provide scent with a minimum of smoke) may be helpful. Don't eat or drink for at least an hour before attempting any practices, as digestion requires energy from the body and so you may feel sleepy as soon as you start to relax.

Relaxation is the first step towards developing a mental space within which meditation or other techniques can be performed. Physically you will need to adopt a position in which your body is composed, i.e. neither strained nor slouching. One position in which this may be achieved is to be seated on a firm chair, with legs together and feet resting flat on the ground. Your head should be upright, hands resting on your lap. A second suitable position is lying down, again with legs together and arms by your sides, hands palms upward. In either event your spine should be straight, maintaining a natural shape without excessive curvature or tension.

Breathing plays an important role in both relaxing your body and mind and assisting concentration. As you sit or lie in the position you have chosen you will need to regulate your breathing. A slow, deep and rhythmic breath pattern should be followed. Begin by experimenting for yourself. Find an appropriate time and get into a suitable position. Focus your attention on your respiration. Try breathing in through your nose and out through your mouth, mentally counting as the breath flows in and out. For most purposes the 2/2 breathing sequence gives best results. This means that you breathe in for a mental count of two and exhale for a count of two.

Working with the Tarot

There are countless ways in which the tarot may be used as an aid for personal development. Meditation on each card, or group of cards, will allow you to investigate the archetypal nature of each. By developing an understanding of each card you will be able to see their natures reflected in your own psyche. By using individual cards as focal images they serve as gateways through which you can explore particular aspects of your own unconscious processes. The key to all these techniques is that through knowledge comes understanding and then power. Your knowledge of the tarot will enable you to access and understand different elements of your self and you will be able to change them as necessary.

A selection of cards may be used to analyse particular elements of any present situation. In this way the archetypal units in the deck serve as a self-counselling aid – describing your situation and offering information as to possible courses of action.

The divinatory use of the tarot is a complex issue and requires dedicated work to perfect, but in the context of personal development there is no reason why the tarot should not also be used as a means of examining past and future situations. What is vital in this practice is to maintain as objective a position as possible. It is all too easy to warp what the cards say, or to allow your intuition to tell you what you would like to hear instead. Reading the cards for other people requires full consideration of moral as well as technical issues. A detailed discussion of divination for others is outside the scope of this particular work; however, by understanding yourself and developing an objective attitude you will find exploration of the tarot for divining or any other 'psychic' ability much easier to cultivate.

The techniques in the exercises below form the basis for using the tarot as a mechanism to assist your own development. As you become more familiar with your own deck, you will be able to evolve your own methods and also be able to refine those given here to suit your personal way of working.

The exercises have various purposes but all involve little preparation or peripherals – all you need is your deck, a quiet time and place and the will to perform them. Remember that they can, and should, be repeated and that you will learn something new every time. Keep a record in your diary or notebook of all information, impressions or ideas presented. None of the following practices is writ in stone; as you develop and learn more, both from other sources and about yourself, you may wish to adapt them.

Drawing Oneself in the Cards

Select three cards from the deck, from any suit or Arcana. The first card should be one that you like as an image. The second should be one that you feel represents you (this may be as you see yourself at present or it may be an image you feel represents your 'inner nature'). The third card should be one that is definitely not you, an image you dislike or that you feel has no part in or relevance to your nature.

Now take three sheets of paper and some drawing or painting materials, whatever you feel happy about using. Draw the cards as well as you can (you don't need to be a great artist to do this). If you wish, adapt or exaggerate any elements of the cards' symbolism in your rendition. As you draw the cards incorporate yourself into each design. If those chosen are court or Major Arcana cards, include your face, hair colour, etc., or perhaps use a passport photograph in the picture. If they are Minor Arcana cards, do the same or incorporate objects that are important or related to you in the design.

Over the course of time you may wish to create your own versions of each card until you have all 78 completed.

Consider how you have drawn each card. What features of the cards are predominant? Which are subdued? How do you feel about your own features being incorporated into the cards? In particular, think about how the image looks on the third card that didn't seem related to you. Spend a while considering the images as though they were from a new tarot pack you had come across. What do these images say to you, or about you?

This exercise can help to demonstrate that each card in the deck represents an aspect of the self. It also provides the opportunity to see just what aspects of each card you consider most important or relevant to you. Remember that these will change – try this exercise again after a month or so and see what differences there are.

Interesting insights into your own psyche can be found by this method. For example, if you depict yourself as Death, this could lead you to consider just how you see your own death, death as a whole, the rebirth experiences in your life, and your own ability to transform any situation. The point here is that by recognition of these powers as being within the self, they can be used productively instead of being repressed or only partially used.

Aspects of the Tarot

Select six cards from your full deck. Choose three deliberately and take the remainder at random.

Look at the first card. Record in your diary or notebook the name of the card. Now, considering the card, write down:

1   a colour
2   an emotion
3   an idea
4   a stage or point in your life

In every case try to get the answers flowing freely. Work by intuition, letting the unconscious provide answers, not the logic of the conscious mind. If you feel the Ace of Wands is a violet card, write that down. It may not correspond to the picture in your deck, or to the colours associated with this fiery suit. However, your answers have meaning for you; they should not be judged right or wrong by anyone else's rationale.

Continue through the cards until you have the four responses from each. Now, letting logic back into the process, look at your answers. What do they tell you about yourself?

The Tarot Story

As with the exercise above, this one will work only if you allow impressions to flow from your unconscious without the intervention of rationalisation. In this exercise a fantasy play is evolved. Such practices as this form the basis of the skills necessary for divinatory use of the tarot proper, and this exercise will stand you in good stead if you want to learn more about this subject.

Take the deck and shuffle the cards thoroughly until you feel happy to start. Don't get apprehensive or self-conscious about the procedure – it is important to approach this exercise in a spirit of fun. You may wish to set up an audio tape to record your words at this point.

Select the first card from the deck. Look at it and begin to develop a story using the card as your springboard. You may wish to use the card's imagery, or your feelings, or ideas that immediately come to mind. For example, if you pick up the Hermit you might begin: 'Once upon a time there was an old man who lived in the hills far away. He liked walking, and every day in the evening he would light his lamp and make his way down the mountain to see the sea ...'

Once you feel that you have got as much as you can from the first card, select the next card and continue the story. For example the Ace of Discs: '... Now as the old man neared the seashore he found a large, round, flat loaf of bread lying on a rock and he wondered who had made such a wonderful loaf ...'

Carry on with your story, using as many cards as you like, until you reach a natural conclusion. When you have finished, recall your story or play back the audio tape. Imagine that the story is new to you, a fairy story or legend from another land. What is the story saying? Is there an underlying moral or point to the tale? Is there any repetition of imagery or words? What does the story tell you about the story-teller, or even the culture he or she comes from?

This exercise can be adapted for use in a group setting where each individual takes one card and continues the story. Alternatively, the whole group could listen to each other's taped stories.

Balancing the Elements

The aim of this exercise is to assist in the formation of a balanced and whole psyche. As explained above, the four Elements may be seen as representing the activities of the self. The process of individuation, or personal development, should not result in a bland, unmotivated psyche. Emotions, such as anger, fear, hatred, love, enjoyment, etc., belong to the psyche of an individual on the road of personal development just like anyone else. What is crucial is that one aspect of the personality should not dominate any other. So when the individual comes across a situation that requires emotional sensitivity, he or she can be sensitive; in a situation where aggression is demanded, this can also be called upon. The ability to shift easily and cleanly between different abilities or properties of the mind is a vital step in understanding the nature of the self.

The aim in this exercise is to stimulate one set of elemental qualities within the psyche to offset an overabundance, or to harmonise with another set. So if you are a person who tends towards too much passivity and emotion, you may wish to strengthen your fiery traits to balance your inherently watery ones. If you are a very practical person but you wish to sharpen your intellectual skills and become a better communicator, you would activate your Air skills to offset a predominantly earthy personality.

To begin with, decide with care which Element, or Elements, you lack. Take your time and try to be as objective as possible about your own nature. Look back over your diary for the past months and see how you have interacted with others and within yourself. Once you have made your decision, prepare a quiet room in which you will not be disturbed. A low level of light is best, and most people find that this exercise is most successfully conducted at night when there is less distraction, and the threshold between conscious and unconscious minds is thinner.

Take out your deck and choose the suit you wish to work with. Select four cards that represent the aspects of the elemental abilities you want to cultivate. Let your intuition guide you in your choice.

Now select one court card or Major Arcana card that you feel represents the characteristics you wish to develop. Spread out the five cards you have selected in front of you as in Fig. 5.

Relax your body and your mind, and breathe in and out using the 2/2 rhythm described on page 30. Now focus your attention on each card in turn, moving your attention from the first to the second card, and so on until you are concentrating on the fifth character in your spread. Now move your awareness to encompass the whole group of cards. Imagine that you are looking in a mirror that shows not your face but aspects of your own inner nature. Mentally identify yourself with the forces each card represents. Spend at least 15 minutes concentrating on this.

The next day, in other ways, try to call to mind the Element you are trying to cultivate. Try to wear colours reminiscent of the Element you are working on, try eating foods, wearing perfumes, or doing activities that are in some way related. For example, if you were working with Fire, you might wear reds, golds and yellows. Try eating spiced foods and red meat, wear warm, rich scents and perhaps begin studying a martial art.

Repeat this practice for at least seven days. If at any stage you find yourself uncertain about the abilities you are trying to cultivate, calm your mind and imagine your pentagram illuminated with the colour of the Element you are working on.

Over the whole of this period, keep a careful note of how well each session of contemplation of the cards has gone, and whether or not the qualities you were looking for came out the following day. Once the seven-day period is over, forget it – even if you don't appear to have had much success. Allow the work you have done to sink into your unconscious. By doing this the new programme your conscious

Figure 5: Balancing the Elements

Major Arcana or court card

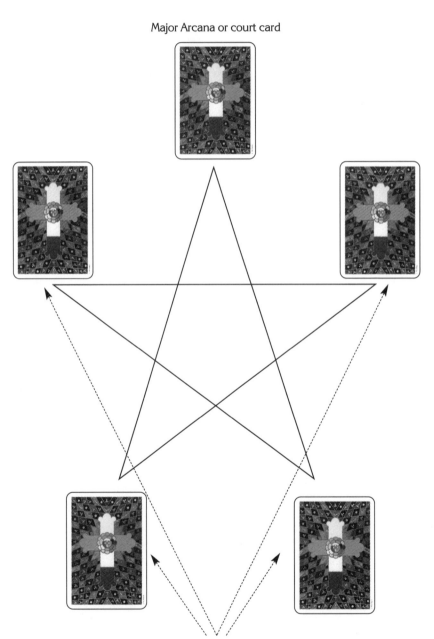

Cards selected from desired Elemental suit

mind has created will act like a seed implanted in the unconscious and will slowly germinate. Even if you do not notice any immediate effects, within a month you should see a definite increase in the abilities or traits you have been working on. If the exercise appears unsuccessful, leave at least three months from your first try before attempting it again.

Again, keep notes on dreams, events and moods in your diary or notebook throughout this period.

Talking and Listening to the Deck

The following exercise is designed to provide you with an opportunity to put your questions or problems to a particular archetypal force within your own unconscious. The second part of the exercise allows your unconscious to reply, to resolve problems, and to provide inspiration or new understanding.

Talking

Go to your quiet room and select the card you wish to communicate with from the deck. You may wish to examine a card that you don't fully understand, or you may wish to pick one that you feel could help with understanding a particular problem.

Relax your body and mind, sit comfortably and use the 2/2 breathing rhythm.

Place the card in front of you and spend a while just looking at it. Observe the colours, the expression of any figure, and the way the whole image is put together.

Now begin to speak. Treat the card as though it were a combination of priest, confessor, psychological counsellor and friend. Begin by introducing yourself to the card, then ask it whatever you want, and explain to it how you feel, what you think, how you see it. It may take some practice but try not to be self-conscious. As with the tarot story exercise above, let your words come naturally, open up your heart and mind. You may want to get angry and shout or to put a complex, intellectual argument to the card – do what you feel is right.

Once you have finished talking to the card, thank it (this may sound silly but it is actually a good way of making an element of your own psyche appear as an objective entity). Place the card back in your deck.

Listening

The following evening take out the card you have already talked to. Place it in front of you in a location where your eyes can focus easily on it, without strain. Once again relax your body and mind. As you sit and observe the card let your mind empty. With every breath you let out, imagine the tension, the frustration, the cares of daily life slipping out of your mind. Look at the card and visualise it not as a two-dimensional card but instead as a window through which you can see a scene in the distance.

Now imagine that you are walking or floating towards the window (you may prefer to close your eyes at this point) and into the tarot card. Feel the sensation of your own movement and be aware that you are entering the archetypal world of whichever card you have selected. As you pass through the perimeter of the card you feel a warm glow – affirm to yourself that you are relaxed, calm and safe.

Now stand or sit before the image in the card. Be aware of the sights, sounds and smells that this aspect of your unconscious projects into your conscious mind. Just be aware and listen. Eventually, the figure in the card may begin to speak, you may hear words in your own head, or you may simply become aware of the answers to your questions forming in your consciousness.

Once you are happy that you have got the maximum experience from the session, feel yourself drifting back, away from the figures in the card. Become conscious of your breathing and the relaxed solidity of your own body. Open your eyes and spend a few moments quieting your mind again. Put away your deck and rest.

This exercise takes some practice to perfect. If you are a visually orientated person you may be very conscious of the imagery around you. On the other hand, you may have a series of definite feelings but little visual imagery. After some practice you may wish to adapt this exercise to suit your own nature better. For instance, you may wish to imagine yourself standing at a door and opening it to reveal the scene of the card.

After an exercise of this type it is advisable to have a little food and drink to return your mind and body firmly to the conscious level of experience. You may also notice a slight drop in body temperature, so have a warm room for your practice. Again, record all results.

Dealing with the Past

Much of the personality rests upon the past experience of the psyche. As modern psychology shows, examining the past can provide useful information on how the individual acts in the present. While there is no way of changing one's past, fantasy plays excluded, it is possible to look back with objectivity at one's history. The following practice is designed to give you the chance to look back into your own past and to see important or difficult events in your life with a fresh and dispassionate eye.

Go to your quiet room and relax your body and mind. Take your deck and hold it in your hands. Mentally count backwards, and imagine that you are rewinding a film of your life until you reach the point you want. (Use whatever method works best for you. Try counting each exhalation and imagining that each time you breathe out you go back in time. Alternatively, imagine a digital clock with the numbers falling backwards, faster and faster.)

Once this is done, shuffle your cards until you feel comfortable that they are shuffled enough. Lay the cards out in three lines as in Fig. 6. Lay out as many cards as you feel is necessary, keeping equal numbers in each line. About four cards in each line is usual.

- Line 1 represents the outward situation
- Line 2 represents you and your own feelings and ideas
- Line 3 represents other players or characters in the situation

Look at the cards spread in front of you. Don't analyse or think, but let your feelings and intuition work for you. (Especially, don't have this or any other book with you! The meaning of the cards should be determined by your own unconscious impressions and not by what any writer says.)

Figure 6: Dealing with the past

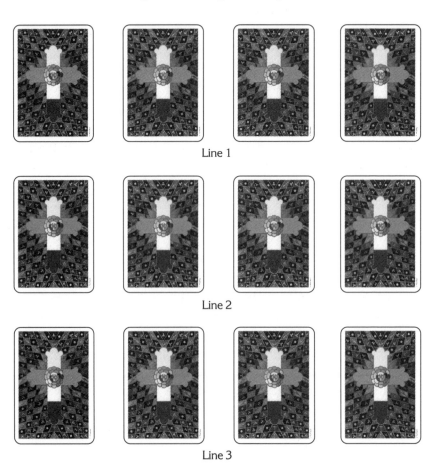

Line 1

Line 2

Line 3

The lines may well represent a progression in time. For instance, you may feel that the left hand side of line 1 shows the beginning of the situation and the last card in that line the conclusion of the situation. As well as looking at the cards as lines across, look at the downward lines formed by the cards in the three lines. These groups may well show how the 'you' (line 2) interacted with the situation (line 1) and others involved at the time (line 3). Spend at least 15 minutes looking at the spread you have developed. Are there characters in line 3 or elements of the situation in line 1 that you didn't consider at the time? How did you interact with the others involved with you then?

Next, become conscious of the 'now' (mentally flick your digital clock forward if you wish). If this were a divination about the future, how would you handle the situation? Would your actions be different and if so in what way? It may be helpful to write down or speak aloud the changes you would make in your actions now that you have had a chance to review the event.

Seeing the Cards in Character

As you become more familiar with your deck, you may wish to look for the symbolism and concepts represented by the deck outside of yourself.

Spend one week looking at the outside world through the medium of the tarot. Look at strangers. What card or elemental qualities do they appear to have? Watch people on television or children playing and relate them to the events taking place. Which units within the tarot are reminiscent of these things? Make notes in your diary and see how best you can apply the symbolism of the tarot to your daily life.

Making your own Ace of Discs

This is an exercise in making affirmations, that is, affirming your ability to do something as much as acknowledging your desire to attain certain goals.

Take a sheet of paper, at least A3 size, and draw a large circle on it. Divide the circle into sections (as many as you like). Label each one, in pencil, with a title. These should be major areas in your life that you would like to improve or develop. An example is given in Fig. 7.

Now take your tarot deck and go through it until you come up with one card to represent each sector. Place these cards around the circle so that each one is by the sector it relates to. Look round the cards and draw one symbol from the card on to each sector. So, if you have chosen the Ace of Cups for the sector marked 'Health', you could draw a cup in that sector (if you want to use paints or different colours feel free to do so). So you now have a disc divided into a series of units and in each unit is a symbol that represents the attainment of fullest benefit for each area of your life. Rub the pencil words off your circle

Figure 7: Making your own Ace of Discs

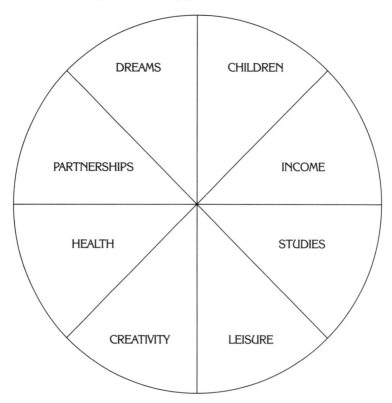

(the aim is to let these symbols drift into your unconscious and, as the conscious mind deals with words, these need to be removed to clarify the imagery).

Hang up the disc in a prominent part of your home (in your bedroom or on the inside of the front door are two good locations). Every day you will see the disc and, even if you do not consciously acknowledge it, the intention you have filled it with will emerge in your unconscious mind.

Try this practice for two months and see what results you obtain. Later, you may wish to add other sectors to the disc in order to develop some other areas of your life.

Chapter 3

Relax, Renew, Revitalise

he exercises in the last chapter use the tarot as a means of personal development. However, there are additional exercises that are not limited to using the tarot which are worthy of study and practice for, if continued over a period of time, they can be tremendously beneficial. Many of the exercises that follow have been primarily derived from various yogic systems. In the western world many life-threatening diseases are thought to be triggered by stress. These exercises will combat the effects of stress and hypertension generated by everyday living.

One vital feature of these exercises is that they should be performed in a consistent, regular way. A parallel can be made with brushing one's teeth: it's is no use scrubbing away furiously for an hour every third day, yet there is every point in brushing effectively and regularly for a minute or two but more often.

Most of the practices given below incorporate a physical component with visualisation. The mental activity of visualisation, or simply conjuring up a feeling, is linked to the physical action of maintaining a regular breathing pattern. This dual action serves to create an effect that occurs in the physical body as well as in the inner levels of the psyche.

As with the study of the tarot, there is no need to subscribe to a particular belief system to use these methods. They are inter-religious just as they are inter-social, applicable and usable by all people of whatever race, age or creed.

The White Light Exercise

The basis of this practice comes from hatha yoga and pranayama (the yogic teaching that uses control and appreciation of the body space as a means to enlightenment, and the science of breathing and the way this affects the mind and body).

You should allow at least 15 minutes for this exercise. You may wish to perform it outdoors or in your own quiet room. In either case your immediate environment should be well ventilated but comfortably warm and free of distractions. Wear loose clothing or even undress.

1 Sit or lie in a comfortable position. Ensure that no part of your body is strained, that your spine is straight and your abdomen unrestricted.

2 Focus your attention on your breathing, making it slow and regular. This exercise seems most effective if breath is taken in through the nose and expelled from the mouth. Spend some time just observing the flow of breath through your body. If other thoughts arise in your mind to distract you, simply return your attention to your breathing and the slow, even cycle it is following.

3 As you breathe in, begin to visualise or feel the air entering you as a radiant white light. As the breath enters your body the light spreads out from your lungs, permeating the whole of your being. Be conscious that the breath is revitalising and relaxing you, unblocking damaged areas of your mind–body complex and refreshing every aspect of your self.

4 As you breathe out, imagine all tension, frustration and impurities departing with the exhalation. You may decide to see this breath as a murky smog which is being released from your body and drifting away.

5 Repeat this cycle of breathing and imagining until you feel quite relaxed and rejuvenated. Towards the end, you may wish to imagine, or may spontaneously become aware of, the breath you exhale being just as radiant as that which you are inhaling.

When you feel happy to do so, stop the visualisation/imagination process, relax and end the exercise.

Becoming Conscious

As human beings grow we develop a number of skills that are chained together to permit us to do any number of tasks. Thus babies start to develop eye-and-hand co-ordination, and in due course reading skills and object memory are added, giving rise, in time, to abilities as diverse as piloting an aeroplane or typing. Many of our abilities become subconscious, and therefore we tend to rely on them and to undervalue them (this is apparent in people who have had strokes and must relearn basic functions, such as walking, with conscious intent).

The following is an exercise in becoming aware of these subconscious functions, slowing down the mind so that they can be appreciated. By doing this the mind–body complex relaxes and becomes more aware of itself and its interrelation with the outer universe.

1 During the day, at any point, stop what you are doing.

2 Become conscious of the activity in which you are engaged. This may be anything from mowing the lawn to making a cup of coffee.

3 Move through the actions you are doing slowly and carefully. As you do so become aware of the sensations surrounding your occupation, silently translating them into words, e.g. 'Now I am picking up the coffee cup and feeling the sheen of the china, cool and smooth. Now I grip the coffee jar and heap a spoonful of coffee into the cup ...'

Body Relaxation

The following exercise is beneficial whether used alone or incorporated as the preliminary preparation for any other meditative or concentration exercises.

Before doing this exercise, read through the text below and familiarise yourself with the process.

1 Make certain the room in which you wish to practise is quiet and comfortable. Lie on your back, with your hands palms upwards and arms resting naturally by your sides. If you wish, a firm pillow may be used beneath the neck to support the head (in hatha yoga this posture is known as the Shiva asana).

2 Focus your attention on your feet. Become aware of the position in which they are resting. Curl up your toes until the muscles are taut, then very slowly relax them and let them lie still. Again curl up your toes until the muscles are tight, and once more relax them slowly. Feel the tension slipping away as your toes uncurl and lie still.

3 Move your attention up your body to your ankles. Pull your feet up to point towards your chin, as far as they will go. Then relax the muscles in your ankles slowly. Repeat this procedure. Now your feet feel heavy, sinking right down. Let the floor support them – be completely relaxed.

4 Move on to your calf muscles; tighten them until your legs feel stiff, then let them go. Relax, feeling the floor supporting the weight of your legs. Then repeat the process.

5 Bring your attention to your knees. Tighten all the muscles around this area. Relax and repeat.

6 Repeat this process with the muscles in your upper legs. Once your legs are totally relaxed, be aware of your lower limbs sinking on to the floor.

7 Focus on your stomach muscles, contract and relax them, and then repeat.

8 Continue this process through your hands, arms, upper body and neck.

9 Again let your body relax, and feel it being supported by the floor.

10 Focus your attention on your facial muscles, jaw, eyes and forehead. Contract each set of muscles in turn, relax and repeat.

11 Now from the top of your head to the soles of your feet feel every muscle relaxed, your body heavy and resting evenly on the ground.

12 Spend as long as you like in this state or go on to some other exercise.

Heightened Awareness

Most people live in a world of sensory grey tones; their sensory system is so cluttered or under-used that they fail to appreciate what is under their noses.

The following brief exercises are intended to make you consider your sensory system, to increase your awareness of your environment and thereby develop a more profound relationship with both external and internal realities.

1 Take an item of food or drink. Place it in front of you and really look at it. Consider its colour, shape and size. As you slowly eat or drink it, turn all your senses upon it. What does it feel like, what is the texture, temperature, smell and taste? How does it feel in your hands or as it is swallowed? Does it make you feel less hungry, revitalised or refreshed?

2 At any point in the day, stop what you are doing. Focus your awareness on the posture of your body. Notice how you are sitting, standing or lying, and whether your body is relaxed or tense, extended or contracted. Now shift your attention to your body's relationship to other objects or people in your environment. Are you sitting close to the door? Leaning close to the person you are with? In the centre of the sofa, or on the edge of your seat?

3 Count the number of times during the day that you mis-hear what people say. Focus your attention on the sounds around you, listening for the hidden sounds that are often missed, such as the ticking of the clock, the hiss of the air conditioning, the rumble of cars on the road outside.

4 Watch the turn of the seasons, the cycles of growth and decay. Observe which plants come into flower first in the year and those that flourish later. Notice how the quality of the air, the sunlight and the wind change day by day.

5 Observe other people around you. When you see a stranger in the street, look at the way he or she walks. How are they dressed? Do they appear confused, happy, sad or relaxed?

In the process of personal development the exercises given above are best interspersed throughout your work with the tarot. In this way one can avoid becoming too enamoured by the cards themselves, forgetting that they are reflections of the universe (both inner and outer) and not intended to be studied in the abstract, insular chamber of a sensory ivory tower.

Chapter 4

Reading the Cards

ivination by the tarot – 'reading the cards', as the process is usually known – is an important aspect of the cards' use. But using the tarot as a divinatory system can also be an excellent method for personal development. When conducting a tarot reading, either for oneself or for another individual, a number of skills are necessary. The primary skill is known as 'organised intuition', which means the ability to receive intuitional impressions from the unconscious and to organise and qualify them with the conscious mind. In order to make this possible, a balance must be struck within the self, and this depends on the correct participation of the ego.

When reading the cards, a non-judgemental, objective approach is necessary. The intuition must be guided by the ego into consciousness and communicated in a way that will be intelligible to oneself or to any other person involved. Having a 'clarified ego' is vital to reading the cards.

For most people the difficulty with approaching the notion of reading is that they suppose that a complex system is required. Some individuals are totally sceptical about the idea of divination, and perhaps even more are confused or concerned that such a feat is at all possible. The key point is that synchronicity provides a plausible theory that allows for the divinatory feature of the cards. It is no more 'illogical' to use synchronistic theory as a working hypothesis for trying the system for oneself than it is to rely on Newton's laws of motion when driving a car. As to the concern some people feel – that knowing the future would be worse than not knowing – this is, on the whole, a groundless worry. The tarot, and indeed any divinatory system, shows not fate but rather the likely courses of action and their effects and situations that may result, depending upon which course the individual pursues. The main feature of tarot divination is not 'seeing the future': instead it is making the questioner aware of the present and the possibilities for the future, and assisting that individual in making honest and productive choices. The tarot does not demand the existence of 'destiny' for divination, any more than it requires one to believe in God before it can be used as a tool for self-exploration.

Tarot Techniques

Most tarot packs contain a short instruction booklet that shows spreads for divination, particular meanings for each card and the meanings of each position within the spread. As already explained, this attitude is misleading. The cards do not have particular meanings, but rather they are complexes of symbols which, like letters in the alphabet, have different meanings in different situations and contexts.

With spreading the cards, as with their interpretation, guidance should come from the unconscious mind, focused by the clarified ego through to consciousness. Limiting oneself to a set series of meanings, keywords or position functions in the spread will produce a mechanical reading that, while it may be accurate, will certainly fail to be personally relevant or able to comprehend issues to which the keywords properly apply.

By carrying out the exercises in Chapter 2, you will have an excellent basis from which to explore reading the cards. You may be able to read for yourself or perhaps you have one or more friends who would allow you to practise with them. In reading for others you should bear in mind the highly privileged position you hold.

Code of Conduct

Tarot reading provides an excellent counselling method and thus, though still a novice, you may well be placed in difficult and sensitive situations even in a 'trial' reading. Very often people will open their hearts and minds when, with a combination of intuitional information and concise communication, they feel you are closer to understanding them than anyone before.

The moral and social issues that surround reading require careful consideration, but some of the basic principles that you would be advised to follow are:

1 Maintain, as far as possible, an objective and non-judgemental attitude.

2 Do not become a chattel to the curiosity or addiction for 'divine guidance' which some seek. Read only when *you* feel ready to do so, in comfortable conditions and for as long as necessary and no more. The exception to this rule is that, even as a beginner, you should not refuse to give a reading to someone who really needs it. You do, however, have the right to refuse to answer any question that might ethically compromise you or to refuse on the grounds that the querent is mentally or emotionally unstable.

3 If you see the possibility of health problems or an accident in the cards, speak positively; advise the querent to take care in these matters, but do not worry them needlessly.

4 With the issue of physical death there is a series of important constraints. The Major Arcana card Death represents a transformation from one state to another and it may well be necessary to explain that this is not physical death that is being prophesied. But in the very unlikely event that you have a definite intuition that the querent will shortly die, you cannot afford to express this. Quite apart from the moral implications (that you may literally scare them to death), it is legally ill-advised to predict the death of another person.

5 Even after years of experience the best readers still get interpretations wrong, or fail to see other possibilities that emerge in a reading. Be aware of this and be sure the querent is too, reminding him or her that a reading examines the present and suggests the future. It does not compel or reflect an intractable fate.

6 Work with the querent. Make certain that the language you are using is intelligible and that the client gives you feedback. The tarot is not a guessing game and any reading works best when both reader and client work together, using the cards as the linking element between them.

7 With virtually no exceptions the confidence of what passes between reader and querent is absolute. Only under the most extreme circumstances (sexual abuse and issues involving physical violence) should the reader even consider releasing information about a reading to a third party. In a more exoteric counselling system there is usually a 'line leader' to unload to but the actual content of a reading remains confidential. You may of course ask the person if they mind sharing information, maybe in order to help them more. Avoid reading for more than one person at a time. In this way the querent may be more confident to speak his or her mind. The confidence rule still applies (even between partners, married or otherwise).

As well as necessitating organised intuition and ego clarification, reading the cards will give you deep insight into human life. Counselling, listening and supporting a querent is, ideally, as much a means of learning more about yourself as it is of discovering the querent's situation. The evidence supports the contention that those people who have studied and used, in a directly interpersonal sense, a divinatory system frequently have a more penetrative understanding of human nature (and therefore their own inner nature) than the aloof, abstract studies of the hermetic mystic.

Preparation for a Reading

You will require the same quiet room conditions for reading as for any of the exercises with the tarot. If you are reading for another person, let him or her relax, offer tea and talk about what that client expects and whether he or she has had a reading before. Establish as much as you can about your client. A good reading is one in which querent and reader work together, qualifying, listening, talking and intuiting, using the cards as the focus of the whole operation. There is no use spending half an hour establishing from the cards that the querent is contemplating marriage when that information could come from the querent to the reader and is known already. The querent may well express the desire to know the answer to a specific question or be advised about a particular area in his or her life. In this instance you, the reader, must remember that even in a practice reading a friend may well ask a superficial question but really want information on a much more profound, and probably private, problem.

The issue of how you should proceed with a reading, for example whether you or the querent should shuffle the deck, is entirely a matter of personal preference. There is no mysterious law that defines a right or wrong way of dealing the cards.

Inversions

If you have read any other information on the tarot, you may well have seen the phenomenon of 'inversion' or 'ill-dignified' mentioned. The idea is that, in a reading, when a card falls inverted (from the view of the reader) its meaning is reversed.

This practice of reading cards as 'upright' or 'reversed' is of recent origin, as evidenced by the fact that many earlier tarot decks are horizontally symmetrical (they look the same either way up), and is inconsistent with the tarot system as a whole. As the meaning of each card depends, ultimately, on one's intuition, it is ridiculous to suggest that Strength when upright means courage, strength, victory, yet when inverted means cowardice, weakness, defeat. This view betrays a simplistic, mechanistic view of the cards. Moreover, the notion that the cards are somehow wrong, evil or adverse if 'ill-dignified' (reversed) harks back to a misunderstanding of duality where negative/positive is confused with moral judgements of good and evil.

Card Patterns

The spreads that follow are suggestions; they are designed to assist the reader by providing a grammar into which the meaning of each card may be apprehended. There is no reason why these, or indeed any spread, cannot be adapted to suit personal taste and experience.

As emphasised before, let organised intuition be your guide in spreading the cards and interpreting what you see in them.

Pentagram spread

This spread uses the symbol of the pentagram as a mechanism of exploring any number of different issues. The four Elemental points of the pentagram mark the card(s) that relate to the areas governed by the Element in question. The fifth card, at the Spirit point, is the figurehead or overture to the other cards, giving a summing up and basis from which to view the whole spread.

During the course of a reading, one might wish to spread two or more pentagrams, perhaps imposed one over the other, to look at different aspects of the querent's situation. Within any spread, the interaction between the cards and the relationship between ideas will be complex. Let your intuition guide you into looking at the multitude of different patterns that exist between the cards and follow those which are most rewarding in generating both your own intuitions and a productive response from the querent.

The position of the cards relates to the Elements but may be seen in a number of different contexts, for example:

Employment level
Earth: income, financial security, location of workplace
Water: emotional relationships with others at work, how employment affects one's emotional state
Air: job opportunities, interpersonal communications
Fire: career development, individual position in the employment structure, motivation
Spirit: an overview of the situation

Psychological and physiological level
Earth: physical health, diet, exercise
Water: emotional relationships, psychic state, dream level
Air: intellectual status, mental stability and prowess
Fire: drive, will, determination
Spirit: an overview of the individual's body–mind considered as a whole

Figure 8: Pentagram spread

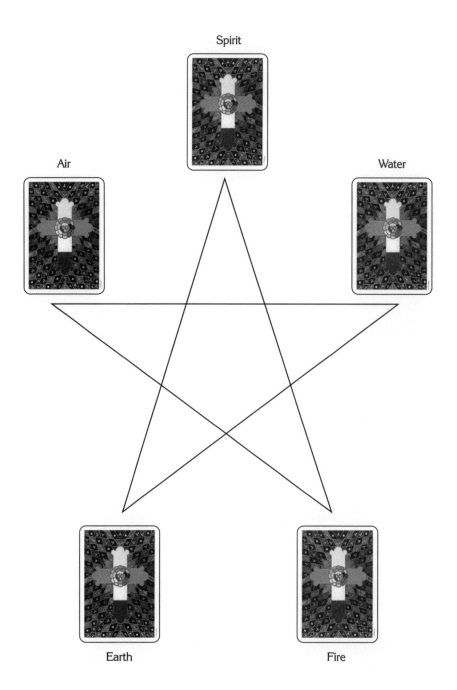

In the two examples on page 54, the positions around the pentagram are related to the appropriate aspect of the life area being examined. Although the reader may have enough inspiration by placing only one card in each position, he or she may wish to lay out more cards for further information. Thus if you don't receive any impression from the card placed in the Fire point of the spread, draw another card (or as many as necessary) until you begin to discern the meaning.

Astrological spread

There are direct relations between the symbolism of the tarot and that of the planets and the zodiac in astrology. For instance, Temperance is related to the sign Sagittarius; the Prince of Cups corresponds to the astrological sector of the 21st degree Libra to the 20th degree Scorpio; the Seven of Discs corresponds to Saturn in Taurus.

The following spread uses the astrological system of 12 houses, each being related to a zodiacal sign. A further ten cards are then placed within the main spread, at random, to give a guide as to the most important areas of the querent's situation.

The ten extra cards relate to the ten planets in astrology: Sun, Moon, Mercury, Venus, Mars, Jupiter, Saturn, Uranus, Neptune and Pluto. To use this spread it is not necessary to have any knowledge of astrology (though it may help). Fig. 9 shows the 12 house cards and the ten extra cards in place; this is an example – the ten inner cards should be put where your intuition guides them. As the reading progresses, you may wish to put out more cards to extend the scope of the reading or delve deeper into a particular aspect.

Each house is accorded a rulership over a particular aspect of human experience; these are as follows:

House 1 – The persona. This house is concerned with self-expression and self-image. It relates to the way others see the querent and their own view of themselves.

House 2 – Persona resources, individual financial security (particularly in the sense of land and property), the immediate effects of individual persona on others.

Figure 9: Astrological spread

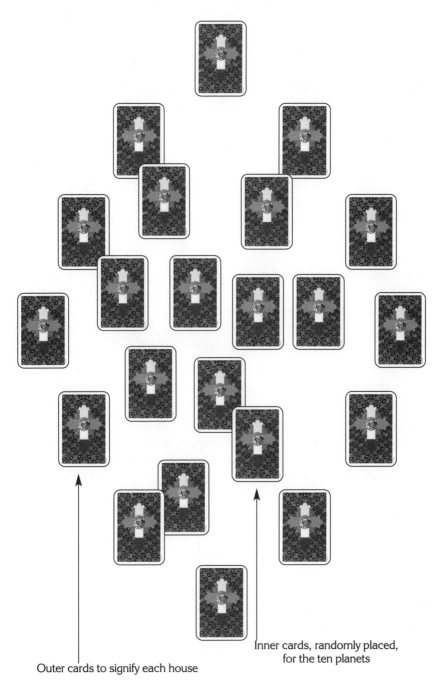

Outer cards to signify each house

Inner cards, randomly placed,
for the ten planets

House 3 – Individual expression and communication; relationships between the individual and the immediate environment. Short journeys and immediate relatives are also under the auspice of this house.

House 4 – Domestic situation, home and family. Psychological foundations of the individual and family, particularly one's parents.

House 5 – Personal creative ability and family resources; one's children (children in this context may be physical offspring or other manifestations of creativity such as books, new projects or business ventures). Romantic life and the flourishing of those resources detailed in the fourth house.

House 6 – Employment, and matters concerned with health. Pets and personal service to other individuals or organisations.

House 7 – The relations between other people and the querent. Business, marriage and other partnerships, as well as the interactions between the individual and those with whom he or she may be in context.

House 8 – The sexual element of the personality. Occult, psychic abilities and interests. Transformation of the self and of others, unconscious desires. Legal matters, inheritance and issues concerned with death (both actual and other 'deaths' such as the end of a relationship or of a protracted situation).

House 9 – Kin, in-laws, religious and moral issues. Long journeys and higher education. The relationship between the individual and the dominant culture or morality of the individual's environment.

House 10 – The public image of the individual. Dominant characters in the formation of the individual's nature (parents, mentors, heroes). The broader implications of one's employment or social status.

House 11 – Friends and associates. Major life changes and crises. The process of broadening one's ideals and social aspirations. Ethics and inspiration.

House 12 – Hidden factors (unconscious forces, akin to those of the 8th house). The individual's ability to overcome entrenched patterns of behaviour and the ability to flow with the natural currents of the universe.

Qabalistic spread

There are also direct correlations between the tarot and the Tree of Life of the Jewish esoteric system, the Qabalah. Each card in the Major Arcana is accorded a letter from the Hebrew alphabet and a 'path' on the diagrammatic representation of the Tree of Life. Each court card and pip card is also related to a 'sphere' on the diagram.

As with the astrological spread, there is no necessity to have a knowledge of the Qabalah. Indeed, it is extremely difficult to obtain currently published and lucid information on this system.

The ten cards are laid down in the order shown in Fig. 10. Once again, additional cards may be put out, if desired, to provide more detail. Cards may also be placed on the main spread to link together the card positions, e.g. a card, or cards, could be placed between cards 1 and 3 to show the link between these two areas. Each point on the Tree of Life has a name that describes its function:

Card 1 (Hebrew *Kether*, meaning 'Crown'). The root of the situation. The inner situation of the individual, projects at their inception, the potential for development.

Card 2 (Hebrew *Chockmah*, meaning 'Wisdom'). Personal initiative, the creating, initialising 'Father' force or archetype. The expression of the individual through the persona.

Card 3 (Hebrew *Binah*, meaning 'understanding'). The nurturing, absorbing, limiting and formulating activity of the 'Mother' force or archetype. Time and gestation.

Figure 10: Qabalistic spread

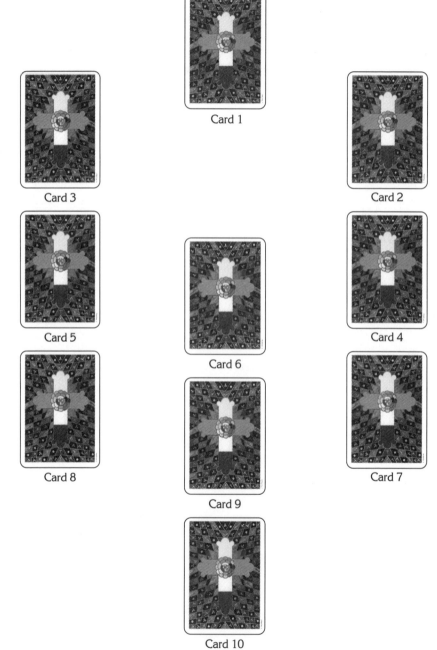

Card 1

Card 3

Card 2

Card 5

Card 4

Card 6

Card 8

Card 7

Card 9

Card 10

Card 4 (Hebrew *Chesed,* meaning 'Mercy'). Expression of the potentials shown in the cards 1 to 3. Financial situation, expression of the individual in society.

Card 5 (Hebrew *Geburah,* meaning 'Severity'). Vital energy, strength of character. Discordant situations, judgement, transformations and breaking out of limitations to discover new order.

Card 6 (Hebrew *Tipareth,* meaning 'Beauty'). The heart of the matter, perceptions of the individual and the way the individual appears to others. Projects accomplished, quests and causes.

Card 7 (Hebrew *Netsach,* meaning 'Victory'). Love and affection. Defence of the self and maintenance of one's individuality. Partnerships and emotion-centred relationships.

Card 8 (Hebrew *Hod,* meaning 'Splendour'). Financial transactions, communication and travel. Intellectual attainments and study. Partnerships and intellect-centred relationships.

Card 9 (Hebrew *Yesod,* meaning 'Foundation'). Mental and physical health, motivations of the self with foundations in the unconscious level. Dreams, sexuality and psychic perceptions.

Card 10 (Hebrew *Malkuth,* meaning 'Kingdom'). The home and the physical circumstances and environment of the individual. Material concerns and family relationships.

Chapter 5

The Major Arcana

0 THE FOOL
Title:
The Spirit of the Aether

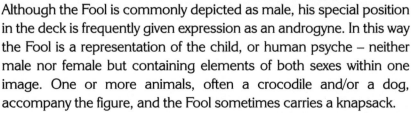

In the vast majority of decks the Fool is shown as a human figure. He is often dressed in exuberant, or even ridiculous, impractical garb.

Although the Fool is commonly depicted as male, his special position in the deck is frequently given expression as an androgyne. In this way the Fool is a representation of the child, or human psyche – neither male nor female but containing elements of both sexes within one image. One or more animals, often a crocodile and/or a dog, accompany the figure, and the Fool sometimes carries a knapsack.

This is a card of light and energy, with the character of the Fool shown walking in an airy dance step. Many decks show him prancing with no apparent concern on the edge of a precipice. This is a card of great wisdom and playfulness. In Hindu doctrine the figure of the Fool can be likened to that of the god Shiva, who dances the ecstasy of creating the universe. As the figure may appear simultaneously as both male and female, so his whole nature is of duality. He is wise and foolish at the same instant, and represents the self on its eternal quest through the myriad experiences of the universe, but there is also an element of trickery and perhaps escapism also. To explain this idea fully, the Fool may be said to describe the irrational forces of the self.

The irrational is, on the one hand, the fanciful dreams of the psyche; it is energy expended in fruitless ways. On the other hand, and paradoxically, the irrational is also the flash of inspiration that manifests as great works of art or new inventions. In both cases it is the unruly activity of the unconscious mind that by-passes logic and provides illuminated insight or illusion.

Personal development with the Fool card

The Fool is the motivating force, depending on the way that motivation is harnessed, and on subsequent experiences the Fool may either unlock the secrets of the self or act as the mental trickster to the unwary.

This card symbolises beginnings, and with them the delicate balance that any project heralds. Like a child, the Fool houses a range of potentials within him which may manifest in any number of ways.

In another sense the reckless figure of this card represents an invitation to 'go with the flow', to participate with joy in every aspect of the universe, and to find wisdom in the sunshine and the secrets of the self in the baying of the dog at his heels. He reminds us to enjoy life, to live it to the full and to seize the day.

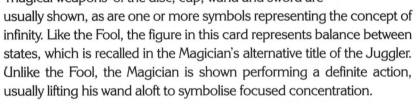

1 THE MAGUS

Title:
The Magus of Power

The Magus, or Magician, stands with the tools of his craft arranged about him. The 'magical weapons' of the disc, cup, wand and sword are usually shown, as are one or more symbols representing the concept of infinity. Like the Fool, the figure in this card represents balance between states, which is recalled in the Magician's alternative title of the Juggler. Unlike the Fool, the Magician is shown performing a definite action, usually lifting his wand aloft to symbolise focused concentration.

The Magician is a card of definite action. In Biblical mythology he represents the Logos, the word of God which, in the beginning, creates the universe. The concept of 'the word' is important as the Magician is also a figure of communication. He stands as the mediator and the controller between the realm of men and the realm of the gods. The Magician also seeks to understand, manipulate and direct the forces of the cosmos in accordance with his own will. As the communicator, the Magician is also a guide through the hidden byways of the unconscious. Through his talent for linking different forces in the psyche, the individual may see, experience and come to terms with painful memories or emotional complexes. He may also open up hidden recesses in which lie talents or wisdom that were previously hidden.

Personal development with the Magus card
The Magus makes us aware of ourselves and therefore of the abilities to heal and to harm that lie within us all. This card represents spontaneity and an injunction to make a decisive action. Standing with a foot in each world – the conscious and unconscious – the Magician symbolises the importance of linking together and of communication between apparently opposed facets in human nature.

II THE PRIESTESS

Title:
The Priestess of the Silver Star

The Priestess is shown enthroned and established in her place of power. Many decks show the figure veiled and seated between two pillars which represent the dual forces (negative and positive) of the cosmos. The Priestess is crowned and the symbol of the Moon is frequently shown on this card.

The Priestess is symbolised by the Moon and water: she displays the characteristics of illusion, enchantment and reflectivity. Like the sea, she has hidden depths, tides and moods that change, though her essential nature remains the same. She is the emblem of pattern and of cycle, with different aspects being apparent at different times (as with the phases of the Moon). Symbolically she is the Virgin; in the context of the tarot's symbolism this implies that she is potential. Whereas the Magician directs his power through the universe, the Priestess invites the universe to act upon her – but she does this 'according to her will'. In one sense she is the unrealised idea that waits until the environment is right to grow: in another sense she is the illusion of the unrealised dream.

She symbolises the infinite potential of the unconscious, which only waits to be fertilised by the consciousness for it to spring into action.

Personal development with the Priestess card
The Priestess signifies that power comes as much from the passive abilities, such as sensitivity and intuition, as from the direct action of the Magician. She is an injunction to look deeper into the self, to look beyond her 'veil' and to see behind layers of conditioning and superficiality.

As a figure of potential she counsels the individual to avoid complacency and to acknowledge the limitless potentials of external situations and the powers of the unconscious mind.

III THE EMPRESS
Title:
The Daughter of the Mighty Ones

The Empress is usually shown enthroned with the symbols of earthly power (royalty). The astrological symbol for Venus is her staff of office and she is shown crowned. Her demeanour is more open than that of the Priestess. Growing plants are commonly shown at the foot of her seat. The device of the eagle is frequently shown on a shield resting on the earth.

The Empress is, superficially, very similar to the Priestess. However, as the Priestess is power hidden, or potential, so the Empress is power overt and manifest. She is the Great Mother who unifies opposite forces in the universe. As a mother she is the vehicle through which power is made concrete in the realm of experience. She is the emblem of riotous creation in nature and, paradoxically, the embodiment of the natural process of destruction.

The Empress represents the emotion of love or attraction that binds together the conscious and unconscious minds even as it connects the lover to the beloved. Her ability to bring anything to fruition depends on this mutual attraction of opposites. In order to create, the Empress, like the physical mother, is able to sacrifice herself – in other words to divide into two, as mother and child.

Personal development with the Empress card

The Empress represents and invokes the creative process in the individual. She synthesises new things through the union of opposites and sometimes even contradictory forces. Her creative function operates without prejudice, and thus she generates both angels and monsters with equal force.

The Empress represents the importance of division as much as she does unification, as the process of creation cannot become complete until the created has become separate from its creator.

IV THE EMPEROR
Title:
The Son of the Morning; Chief among the Mighty

The Emperor is shown with symbols of royalty; sometimes he is depicted resting against his throne in a posture reminiscent of the way in which young men hang round street corners. He holds a staff of office and, as with the Empress, the symbol of the eagle is common to this card.

As the Empress is nature, so the Emperor is society, which imposes its own brand of order on nature. His stability depends on the continuity of nature; without it, his fiery disposition would result only in swift and angry action. As an emblem of authority his is the first image of human consciousness in the tarot, far more accessible to rational thought than the Empress.

The Element of fire is closely associated with the Emperor. This Fire is the binding agent of society, the rousing cry of the battle leader, and the motivating 'community spirit' of any group. The Emperor is the will. He may be seen in contemporary society as the ambitious executive or the dedicated scientist. On the other hand, he is also the dictator or military general.

Personal development with the Emperor card
The Emperor suggests the use of logic to understand the mechanism of the self. However, as he is reliant on the Empress, he does not deny the importance of feeling.

This card represents the determination of the individual on the quest for self-understanding, and orders the process of personal development so that emotion and intuition may be qualified by conscious thought and maximised. He is also the thirst for knowledge that may be used in understanding the self.

V THE HIEROPHANT
Title:
The Magus of the Eternal Gods

In many decks the Hierophant is depicted as a religious master (and is frequently titled 'The Pope'). He holds a staff of office denoting his religious or spiritual authority rather than the 'temporal' power of the Emperor. Two human figures are often shown standing before him.

The Hierophant is establishment and authority. This is the first card to move away from the directly personal towards the social. Classically, as the Pope or religious leader he was the spiritual and secular law that provided the moral fabric of human society. The character of the Hierophant mediates between the realms of men and the gods, yet, unlike the Magus, the Hierophant communicates in an ordered way. His knowledge, the interaction between the human and the archetypal, comes in the form of dispensation and teaching rather than direct revelation or mystical ecstacy.

Personal development with the Hierophant card
The Hierophant represents the first step into conscious interaction between the archetypal unconscious and the personality of the individual. He depicts the necessity for an ordered way to be found whereby the personal revelation of the self may be expressed in an outward form.

He also represents the importance of developing a moral or belief system through which the expression of the 'inner nature' may find fulfilment. The importance of continuity, tradition and renewal is expressed here.

VI THE LOVERS
Title:
The Children of the Voice;
Oracle of the Mighty Gods

Commonly two humans are shown standing before a larger or shrouded figure. Chequered colouring is often used to recall the interaction of positive and negative forces in this image. In many decks a winged Cupid, bow drawn, is shown above the whole scene.

The Lovers card, often referred to as the Brothers, represents the dynamic unification of different human qualities. In the card the masculine and feminine qualities of the human psyche are linked. Importantly, these are qualities, not genders – many packs show two women or two men.

The figure presiding over the marriage is the Hierophant, who signifies how the mercurial process of mediation of relationship between conscious and unconscious has become humanised.

By unifying the masculine and feminine aspects of the self the psyche forms a new centre. From this new centre, the Lovers may move in any direction, becoming passive or active, intellectual or emotional as the situation demands. In any event, the balance of the whole system is maintained.

Personal development with the Lovers card
The marriage in the Lovers is between the masculine and feminine characteristics of the self. It is only by the unification of the elements within the psyche that the individual can create an integrated whole which is then able to adapt to new circumstances. Rather than looking for the balance of the self in others, the Lovers card counsels that the individual must attain this balance within, otherwise interpersonal relationships will be attempts to find solace in others for those parts of the psyche that have been neglected.

VII THE CHARIOT

Title:
The Child of the Powers of the Waters; Lord of the Triumph of the Light

In the majority of decks, a human figure is shown seated in a chariot pulled by creatures representing the four elemental forces. The charioteer does not appear to strain in controlling the direction of his passage.

The Chariot is a symbol of change and movement; it is a glyph of the cyclic evolution of the universe. The elemental beasts that pull the chariot represent the four complementary energies in the cosmos which, by unified interaction, generate movement. The charioteer maintains an easy balance in his carriage and is confident in his quiet control of the forces around him.

His confidence is an important feature of this card. He is in harmony with his own inner nature and may perhaps feel somewhat self-satisfied. However, the charioteer may only relax because he is aligning his own will with the universal will. The nature of the psyche is to develop towards 'individuation'. This is a feature of the universe, and while the individual may accelerate or become conscious of this process it is not solely dependent on those facts.

Personal development with the Chariot card

The Chariot affirms that the process of personal development is not something that is controlled by the self. Instead, it is a feature of the universe. Conscious personal development may be enhanced or accelerated, but for this to be successful the individual psyche must work hand in glove with the psyche of the cosmos.

The card affirms the importance of maintaining a balance in the self (as shown in the Lovers card), for by maintaining this state the individual is able to work with the forces of the universe. If this is ignored then only frustration, stagnation and stasis will result.

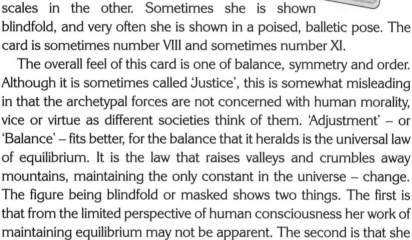

VIII
ADJUSTMENT
Title:
The Daughter of the Lords of Truth; Ruler of Balance

This card is usually shown as a woman holding a sword in one hand and a set of scales in the other. Sometimes she is shown blindfold, and very often she is shown in a poised, balletic pose. The card is sometimes number VIII and sometimes number XI.

The overall feel of this card is one of balance, symmetry and order. Although it is sometimes called 'Justice', this is somewhat misleading in that the archetypal forces are not concerned with human morality, vice or virtue as different societies think of them. 'Adjustment' – or 'Balance' – fits better, for the balance that it heralds is the universal law of equilibrium. It is the law that raises valleys and crumbles away mountains, maintaining the only constant in the universe – change. The figure being blindfold or masked shows two things. The first is that from the limited perspective of human consciousness her work of maintaining equilibrium may not be apparent. The second is that she is a representative of natural order, which works in accord with her 'inner nature' rather than any rational construct.

Personal development with the Adjustment card

Adjustment recognises the intimate, inextricable relationship between cause and effect. The key for the individual is to see that each action, however slight, affects every part of the universe. To place oneself in the role of Adjustment is to acknowledge and become conscious of this fact, to realise that there can be no blame or grace but only an infinite series of actions and reactions. To realise and rejoice in the harmonious interaction of self and not-self, conscious and unconscious, requires great moral courage and a perception of the flexible adjustment principle rather than the narrow justice of human 'fair play'.

IX THE HERMIT

Title:
The Prophet of the Eternal; Magus of the Voice of Power

The figure of the Hermit is generally shown as a robed man holding a burning lamp. He is a wise, withdrawn traveller whose bent and cloaked form suggests a turning inward and secrecy. A walking staff is sometimes shown reaffirming his role of wayfarer.

The Hermit is concerned with inner wisdom. Therefore his journey leads him into the wilderness, perhaps the isolated landscape of the vision quest but, more exactly, the inner reaches of his own psyche.

His shrouded and gentle exterior belies his steely determination to seek out that which is the focus of this quest. The Hermit carries his light with him. This recalls the fact that the light (literally the 'illumination') is something that dwells within him. His introverted, meditative nature is also something of a preparation for emergence into the world once his work is accomplished. The Hermit is the singularity, the seed that, once recognised and activated, may grow and flourish.

Personal development with the Hermit card
The Hermit recalls the importance of looking within the self, of self-examination and contemplation rather than seeking answers outside the self. The light from his lamp shines to illuminate his own quest and, in doing so, he indirectly illuminates the lives of others. This reminds individuals that the greatest good they can do for any other person is to be a fully integrated being.

X FORTUNE

Title:
The Lord of the Forces of Life

The most frequent rendition of the Fortune card is of a wheel which is shown spinning. At various points around the wheel, figures representing the cosmic forces are lifted up or cast down. In any depiction the ideas of rotation, of intermingling and of cycle are vital.

The cyclic form of the wheel creates a mandala image of the universe's progress through innumerable states, over and over without end. As a wheel it is a symbol of equality where each different state is dependent on those that go before it and necessary for those that follow. It is an image of evolution and regeneration.

There is something capricious, if only from the perspective of human consciousness, about the wheel's motion. Like Adjustment, the force symbolised is beyond human morality, yet there is something of the cosmic joker in this card. It is as if the whole universe were the mere plaything of some mirthful deity. Certainly it suggests that the best appreciation of the cosmos is to be had by considering it with a laughing, wry humour.

Personal development with the Fortune card

The wheel affirms that movement from any state to any other state is possible – a cup that is empty can only be filled. The wheel does not suggest a blindly fatalistic attitude. Instead, it suggests a playful attitude to the quest of understanding the self and life in general (certainly play is one of the activities in which learning most readily takes place).

A further point to consider is that in its cycle the wheel describes a spiral. Thus when the individual returns to what appears to be the same point in life it becomes apparent that the return is actually at a different level, or in a different role.

XI LUST

Title:
The Daughter of the Flaming Sword

On this card a woman is shown with a lion (or some other beast). The lion rests against her or she is shown holding its jaws open. Yet there is no sense of effort in her actions. In cards where she is shown bridling or riding the beast there is the same relaxed position, reminiscent of the Chariot. This card is either number VIII or number XI.

The woman in Lust or Strength, represents the feminine nature of the psyche, mediating between the chaotic, instinctive, unconscious level, which cannot be constrained, and the logic of the masculine intellect. The feminine element uses her passivity to form a channel through which energy may flow. The very existence of the conscious mind is fuelled by the passionate forces of the unconscious. By opening herself to these powers, the woman in the card creates a relationship between different strata of the mind, which benefits the whole system.

Vitally she does not seek to change the nature of the 'beast', any more than the vessel seeks to change the liquid poured into it. In Lust the instinctive passions of the unconscious are harnessed so that they may fuel, rather than be at odds with, the rational, masculine qualities.

Personal development with the Lust card

Lust shows that the instinctive elements of the self must be harnessed through the feminine ability to relate and communicate. The 'beast' within the individual is as valuable in the work of individuation as any other part of the psyche and must not be neglected.

The instinctive aspect is a link between the individual and the creative/destructive forces of nature as a whole. The beast is a very potent force, when correctly appreciated and applied.

XII THE HANGED MAN

Title:
The Spirit of the Mighty Waters

The Hanged Man is shown as a figure, usually male, suspended by one leg from a tree or similar object. He hangs head down but rarely seems concerned by his situation. There is a profound sense of relaxation in the majority of depictions.

This is a card of initiation, of moving from one state to another. The Hanged Man is closely related to the Element of Water. He represents the quintessence of Water, the Element of change which must be embraced, rather than fought against, if the process of initiation is to be successful.

This is a card of waiting. In Norse myth, the Hanged Man is the god Odin, who hung for nine days on the World Ash Tree in order to receive the knowledge of the magical runic alphabet (from his own unconscious). The Hanged Man shows that there are points in the life of the individual where inactivity is necessary, where waiting, allowing the self to float upon the waters of the unconscious, can provide new insight.

Personal development with the Hanged Man card

The Hanged Man counsels meditation and also the importance of taking a deliberately undirected course. The individual must allow emotions, thoughts and ideas to flow through the self, without restraint. It is necessary to relax, to float and go with the tides of the self, letting the unconscious mind provide new revelation to the consciousness. The Hanged Man expresses the idea that the secrets of the self are not open to grasping but rather to calm discovery, recognition and then acceptance.

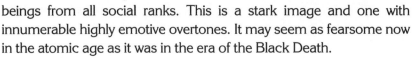

XIII DEATH

Title:
The Child of the Great Transformers; Lord of the Gates of Death

This card invariably shows a dancing human skeleton carrying a scythe. Around the central figure lie the fallen limbs of human beings from all social ranks. This is a stark image and one with innumerable highly emotive overtones. It may seem as fearsome now in the atomic age as it was in the era of the Black Death.

The real meaning of Death is that of change and, while the image is related to the fact of human mortality, its core symbolism is far more subtle and important.

Death is a card of transformation; it heralds great and sweeping change before a new state can be achieved. The idea of putrefaction is of great importance in this symbol. This is a transfiguration from one state to another. Before any new system may evolve, the basic elements of the old system must be broken up. A biological example is the degrading of plant and animal matter to form the fertiliser for new growth. Only by the complete breaking down and cutting back of the old psyche may the essence of a new state of self-awareness flourish.

Personal development with the Death card
Death counsels the individual to accept that the old must be banished before the new can develop. It reaffirms that all loss, as it may appear, is only a stage in the cyclic progression of the universe. Moreover, regeneration and transformation of the old mean that nothing is truly lost; instead it is reabsorbed and reborn in a new and richer form.

XIV ART

Title:
The Daughter of the Reconcilers; Bringer Forth of Life

In this card a human figure, usually a woman, is shown mingling the liquid from two vessels. The mixing of two fluids is central to the symbolism of this card. There are shades of both the Lovers and Justice in this image, which is balanced and harmonised in most renditions.

Art, or Temperance, reunites different elements in the self or universe and places them in their proper order. She mingles together the elements of the self and distils from this mixture a new balance or equilibrium. As with the tempering of steel, by balancing, joining and evening out the composition of a metal it becomes stronger and more durable.

In alchemical symbolism, Temperance represents the continual intermingling of solar (masculine) and lunar (feminine) energies. She is also the strength of cycle, such as the hydrostatic cycle in the earth. By developing a cyclic pattern the system, be it the self or a planet's atmosphere, becomes simultaneously more subtle, complex yet robust.

Personal development with the Art card

Art represents the importance of developing an integrated flow within the self. In other words, communication must exist between the conscious and unconscious minds, and this flow must be carefully regulated. In esoteric languages, Temperance warns against confusing one's levels of reality, i.e. mistaking the dream world for the waking world, and vice versa. Further, she asserts that by developing this harmonious interplay of elements the overall strength of the psyche is enhanced. This leads to the understanding that diversity is strength, and that all things are, essentially, one.

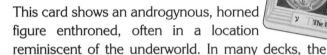

XV THE DEVIL

Title:
The Lord of the Gates of Matter; Child of the Forces of Time

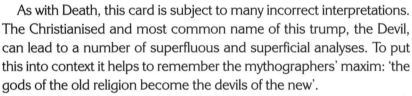

This card shows an androgynous, horned figure enthroned, often in a location reminiscent of the underworld. In many decks, the Devil image is attended by two or more human figures, sometimes chained or linked in some material way to the central character.

As with Death, this card is subject to many incorrect interpretations. The Christianised and most common name of this trump, the Devil, can lead to a number of superfluous and superficial analyses. To put this into context it helps to remember the mythographers' maxim: 'the gods of the old religion become the devils of the new'.

In this card the polarity of masculine and feminine forces, shown in previous trumps, becomes fully manifest. The Devil is associated with the material world, the body of the individual and his or her sexuality. Mythologically, the Devil is the lord of life, of human sexuality, or fertility, and reproduction at a physical level.

An important feature of this image is that he links both heaven and earth – 'as above, so below', as the ancient astrologers put it. The Devil rejoices in creation in all its manifestations.

Personal development with the Devil card
The lesson of the Devil is that the individual must discover the delights of all levels of reality (in Greek myth, he is Pan, whose name means 'all'). As a god of nature, he counsels that rapture, insight and understanding can come as much from the most basic of physical things as it may come from holy texts or long hours of solitary meditation. The Devil also advocates enjoyment both as a means to personal development and as a necessary catharsis to prick the balloon of self-centred or holier-than-thou egotism.

XVI THE TOWER
Title:
The Lord of the Hosts of the Mighty

Most interpretations of this image show a high tower. Streaks of lightning or fire fall from the sky and set the tower alight, causing it to rupture and come crashing down. Often two or more human figures are shown falling from the top of the building.

The Tower is a symbol of stability and permanence. Perhaps the original Tower was the lord's castle that overlooked most medieval towns; this was an image of establishment, the unchanging social order and, probably, repression. This building appears to be as much a prison as it is a refuge – certainly the emotions of the falling figures are hard to judge.

Once more this card asserts that *everything* in the universe must change. The Tower may be built of strong stone yet it yields to a bolt from the blue. The lightning is of importance. In one sense the fire from heaven represents a 'flash' of inspiration that destroys the established orthodoxy (this may be social, as with the impulse to revolution, intellectual, or within the context of personal development). The destruction of the Tower may mean, for a time, weakness (there is no longer any protection), yet there are great opportunities for growth. All walls or limitations are crumbled away so that ignorance may yield to knowledge.

Personal development with the Tower card
This card prompts an examination of one's position: security versus uncertainty; comfort versus adventure. It promotes a confrontation with our fears, as a ride on a roller-coaster raises the adrenalin levels, producing fear and heightened physical awareness. The experiences faced in the Tower raise our psychic levels to a new awareness of our

own position and outlook. The Tower suggests the importance of inspiration as a means of overturning the established order, or perception of the individual. The Tower shows that the containment or barriers that exist within the self are there to serve the individual; they should not be the walls of confinement or limitation.

XVII THE STAR

Title:
The Daughter of the Firmament; Dweller between the Waters

The Star generally shows a woman pouring two vases of liquid into a pool and on to the earth at her feet. She stoops gracefully and gently to unload her store while above her shine one or more stars in the night sky. Organic growth – flowers, trees and animals – is often shown around the central figure.

In many decks, the woman shown in the Star is the first naked human figure. She is stripped of all pretension and the social persona or mask. The Star shows the emergence of a seed of awareness within the depth of inner space. This card shows a far more conscious approach to the purpose of individuation; the Star is both the centre of the self and a point of reference (as physical stars are to navigation) for the development of the self. The figure in this card sits outside in the natural world, the stars above her recall her place in space and time, and she is able to interact creatively with nature by fertilising the waters and the earth with the liquid she carries. In this respect the Star shows the individual as consciously participating in the work of creation; the self is part of the archetypal symphony, a player rather than an observer or unknowing focus of these forces.

Personal development with the Star card

The Star recalls the importance of finding a central point of reference within the self. It suggests that from such a point a creative relationship may be formed between the individual consciousness and the archetypal unconscious. However, the messages from the unconscious should not be accepted without question or analysis.

The Star shows how the process of individuation does not lead to a submergence of individual identity but rather to a clarification of it by relating each aspect of the self to every other – independence is achieved only by understanding interdependence.

XVIII THE MOON

Title:
The Ruler of the Flux and Reflux; Child of the Sons of the Mighty

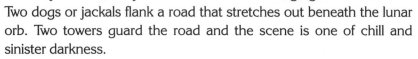

The Moon is generally shown floating above water from which a creature – variously a crab, crayfish or beetle – is emerging.
Two dogs or jackals flank a road that stretches out beneath the lunar orb. Two towers guard the road and the scene is one of chill and sinister darkness.

The Moon is the shadowy analogue of the conscious self. It is concerned with the deep levels of the unconscious that can be penetrated only by non-rational processes.

The Moon is concerned with the cyclic tides of the self that flow through all levels of the individual. The femininity of this card is reaffirmed by this image, as is the lunar cycle that provides the matrix upon which the menstrual cycle is founded. The physical Moon rules the ebb and flow of body fluids and biorhythmic tides. The Moon of the tarot continually changes, having different aspects (symbolised by the phases of the moon), yet there is a continuity in the system – the moon shows different faces, is changing but eternal.

Personal development with the Moon card
The Moon counsels the individual to recognise the cycles that exist within the self and to use these cycles constructively. There is also an affirmation that the flux and flow of the unconscious is formed in discernible patterns, but in order to appreciate these patterns participation rather than analysis is necessary. Acceptance of the forces of the deep unconscious is notoriously difficult, resulting in 'moon madness' or lunacy if the conscious mind rejects the insights of the unconscious. As with the tides in the ocean, these forces can swamp the self if ignored. But they can also provide ideal tides to launch the ships of self-discovery.

XIX THE SUN
Title:
Lord of the Fire of the World

The Sun, usually with a smiling countenance, is shown radiating light over two figures. These figures are generally two children, one male and one female, who are shown playing, leaping or holding hands. The terrain on which the figures stand is green and verdant; they stand outside a protective wall. The overall impression of this card is one of light and joy.

The Sun is the life-giving force, the centre of our lives and of the solar system. The seed of awareness that was developed as the Star now fills the whole sky. The joy of the children under the Sun is that of being able to throw off all the restrictions of cold (psychologically all shackles of the ego) and bask in the sunshine of self-awareness. Here the archetypal intervention in the life of the psyche is as direct as it was in the Tower, but it is not threatening. The Sun is the illumination, literally the bringer of enlightenment. Once again the delight of the children in the sunshine recalls the Star, where the self is a participator in the natural flow of the universe rather than an unknowing pawn subject to its action.

The Sun warms and ripens the relationship between the two figures. They might be taken to represent the masculine and feminine forces of the psyche which have passed into a state of harmony.

Personal development with the Sun card
The Sun shows that by emerging from the apparently safe enclosure of the ego, the self is able to bathe in the radiance of the harmonious interaction of conscious and unconscious. If the individual remains shut away behind protective barriers this greater freedom and the ability to see things 'in a new light' will not be possible.

The Sun shows that, free of restrictions, human consciousness may flourish and the unconscious, once perceived as hidden, dark byways of the mind, may in fact illuminate the relationship between the individual and nature (both inner and outer).

XX THE AEON
Title:
The Spirit of Primal Fire

Most early decks show an angel sounding a trumpet over three naked human figures, one of which may be seen rising from the tomb. More contemporary renditions of this card vary considerably but often the motif of rebirth, especially through fire, is expressed.

This card is often called 'Judgement', though it is rather a poor title, unless it is understood that it is the self that judges the self. This is a card of initiation. While the angel blows the reveille the figures rise (in Christian myth) by their own virtue or grace. The 'Primal Fire' with which The Aeon is associated represents the 'quantum leap' when the psyche has completed one cycle of development, integrated past experiences and emerged into a new state. An excellent metaphor for the initiation described would be that of the butterfly emerging from its chrysalis, a changed being whose history began with its caterpillar existence.

The Aeon also initiates a new cycle of development and, as the penultimate card of the Major Arcana, it shows that individuation is primarily a *process* rather than a progression with a definite start and goal.

Personal development with The Aeon card

This card shows the importance of integrating all elements of the self. To 'like yourself' is a natural precursor to 'know thyself'. The Aeon shows that the individual must be aware that he or she has emerged anew from the cycle that the previous cards represent. Moreover, there is a directive to continue this process, that individuation is a continuum of experience, refining and re-establishing, and this 'deliverance' comes with an acknowledgement of the joyful dance of creation and destruction implicit in all levels of existence.

XXI THE UNIVERSE

Title:
The Great One of the Night of Time

In this card a woman is depicted dancing, sometimes covered with a length of fabric. Depending on the deck, she is either holding two wands or is entwined with a snake. The symbols of the four Elements are shown around the border of the card: the Eagle represents Water; the Lion, Fire; the Man, Air; and the Bull, Earth. Often a garland is shown surrounding the figure of the woman.

The Universe, or the World, is completeness. In this card the four Elements have become creatures and support an image of the self at their centre. In this symbol we see the unification of everything and nothing, 'as above, so below' and the 'dissolve and recombine' of the alchemists.

The floral garland within which the woman dances often resembles a gateway or entry to the womb, implying that rebirth of the self is necessary. The woman is therefore also the baby awaiting birth, but since she is shown as an adult, she is prepared for birth and is conscious of the process.

The woman in the World card dances; she is akin to Shiva in Hindu mythology who sustains the world by his movement. The subatomic vibration and celestial wheeling of galaxies are aspects of this dance.

Personal development with the Universe card

The Universe shows the individual preparing to be born, with full awareness, into a greater state of being. This does not imply entry into some heavenly state but rather the opportunity to embrace a new world, a new cycle of experience, conscious of what has gone before.

The overall process of the Major Arcana, expressed as one within the Universe card, is of developing the 'freedom to move and the freedom to be moved'. That means establishing the harmonious and productive interplay of conscious and unconscious. Carl Jung says of this process:

> *The widened consciousness is no longer that touchy, egotistical bundle of personal wishes, fears, hopes, ambitions which always has to be compensated and corrected by unconscious counter-tendencies; instead, it is a function of relationship to the world of objects, bringing the individual into absolute, binding and indissoluble communion with the world at large. The complications arising at this stage are no longer egotistic wish conflicts, but difficulties that concern others as much as oneself.*

Chapter 6
The Minor Arcana

 he cards of the Minor Arcana are often accorded much less analysis or discussion than that which they so richly deserve. The main reason for this seems to be that the range of 22 picture cards of the Major Arcana are such obviously archetypal figures, complete in themselves, that the Minor Arcana seems something of a poor postscript. In fact the Minor Arcana, both the court cards and pip cards, underpins the very existence of the Major Arcana. One way to understand this would be to look at a magnificent building. Taken overall it may be an impressive structure, yet its existence is dependent on the working interrelationships of hundreds of humble, not so majestic, bricks.

The court cards are often said to describe particular human personalities, or even to stand for individuals with a certain hair or eye colouring. It might be truer to say that each court card represents the way in which the four Elements may manifest, particularly in the context of human nature. The 16 court cards are prototypes, each one representing a combination of elemental forces. In one sense each individual contains the nature of each court card within the self. The work of personal development is to understand, integrate, and be able to shift from one personality or mode of operation to another, as required. The pip cards represent how the elemental forces may be applied, either by the universe at large, or by the individual.

What is important is that *all* these cards are part of the tarot deck; no one card, of any Arcana or sub-set, is any more important than any other. They are all needed, together, to create a whole system.

Most modern decks use a feminine title rather than 'Page' for the last court card in any set. Here we have used the Knight, Queen, Prince, Princess titles that are used in the Thoth tarot, on which the brief descriptions are based.

THE KNIGHT OF WANDS

Title:
The Lord of the Flame and the Lightning; King of the Spirits of Fire

Element: *Fire of Fire*

The Knight appears to be seated on horseback, crowned and often bearing a sceptre or club. Flames are often shown, and the overall impression is of an imperious king, perhaps ready for battle.

The Knight represents the most fiery and unstable characteristics in the human psyche. He is the valiant leader of an army into battle or the tyrannical murderer. This card is the inspiration and incitement to action; he is the drive to *do,* the impulsive action without deliberation. He is the impulse to save the life of a drowning man, or to riot.

The force represented in this card is not easily tempered or formulated. The Knight must have something to act upon; he is the rapturous inspiration of the artist, but a canvas and skill is required if the fire of inspiration is to manifest. If the Knight of Wands is to be successful he must have the correct media to act through: if he does not then he is apt to become 'divided against himself', and the passion of his fire becomes dissipated or impotent.

The Knight of Wands represents human characteristics such as unpredictability, impetuosity, frantic activity, pride and swiftness.

Personal development with the Knight of Wands card

The message of the Knight of Wands is that impetuous, even rash and revolutionary action is a necessary element in the psyche and in human action. However, the card shows how an appropriate focus must be provided if such swift and unstable powers are to come to realisation. This card also shows that human emotions and states are amoral in themselves and that the 'passion' of this card can manifest in innumerable ways.

THE QUEEN OF WANDS

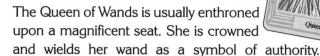

Title:
The Queen of the Thrones of Flame
Element: *Water of Fire*

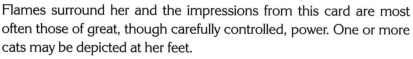

Queen of Wands

The Queen of Wands is usually enthroned upon a magnificent seat. She is crowned and wields her wand as a symbol of authority. Flames surround her and the impressions from this card are most often those of great, though carefully controlled, power. One or more cats may be depicted at her feet.

The symbolism of this card is closely linked to the cat, an animal of ferocious power, but also of elegant and even mysterious restraint. The Queen of Wands is able to move rapidly from a state of active aggression to one of relaxed quiescence.

Character traits linked to this card are those of persistence, generosity, fierceness and possessiveness, or at least protectiveness, of her territory and authority.

The Queen of Wands is a much steadier form of the Knight. She has constrained his fiery force into a regular direction of action. She will defend her established position and, like a cat, maintain her course with savage determination. Such determination may lead to obstinacy and to situations where she may 'cut off her own nose to spite her face'.

Personal development with the Queen of Wands card

The Queen of Wands demonstrates the need for setting one's own limitations. Determination is laudable, but not at any cost. This card also demonstrates the need to accept one's power at all levels of existence. Each individual has power, whether it be to heal or to end the life of another person. However, the strength and authority of the

Queen of Wands is drawn from knowing herself. This recalls the axiom that no matter how much temporal power any one person has, it is useless unless that power is rooted within an integrated psyche. (Adolf Hitler is a prime example of a man who had great personal and temporal power but was unable to reconcile his outward position with his inner weaknesses, and so his determination became his own damnation.)

THE PRINCE OF WANDS

Title:
The Prince of the Chariot of Fire

Element: *Air of Fire*

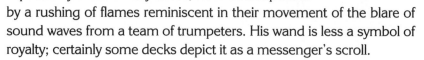

The Prince of Wands may be shown as a youth seated within a chariot. The chariot is pulled by a cat or fiery horse; he is accompanied by a rushing of flames reminiscent in their movement of the blare of sound waves from a team of trumpeters. His wand is less a symbol of royalty; certainly some decks depict it as a messenger's scroll.

As Fire is the Element of passion and will, and Air is the force of communication and swiftness, so the Prince of Wands combines these qualities – he is the messenger, the inspirer. He carries action and transmits it through intelligence. This card is the card of the legal advocate, reporter or politician. He marshals together intellectual information, feeds it a generous dash of passion, even emotivity, and communicates the resulting mix to his audience. An important feature of the Prince of Wands is that he acts as a transmitter; although he may carry his message powerfully its words may not touch him at all. In this sense he is a catalyst to action, supremely enduring but not himself affected by the situations he creates. The Prince uses his abilities to stimulate others to action. There are no Earth qualities in this card – the Prince may organise the workforce but is not directly a part of it.

The qualities of this card are indifference, ambiguity, trickery, swiftness, impulsiveness and expressiveness.

Personal development with the Prince of Wands card

The Prince of Wands shows how any issue or statement has at least two sides to it. He is the master of adaptation, evasion and expression and demonstrates that it is not so much what one believes to be true that matters, as how one believes it. This card counsels the importance of not just appreciating views other than one's own but of exploring and understanding them. Cynicism and ambivalence may provide a bird's eye view from which to observe the world (and one's own actions). However, this is a technique that should not be allowed to become a habit.

THE PRINCESS OF WANDS

Title:
The Princess of the Shining Flame;
Rose of the Palace of Fire

Element: *Earth of Fire*

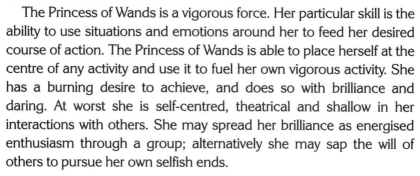

The figure on this card is admirable in the true sense of the world. The Princess is a shining figure frequently shown dancing in flames.
Her wand is an emblem of royal power and also a baton of command, akin to a conductor's baton.

The Princess of Wands is a vigorous force. Her particular skill is the ability to use situations and emotions around her to feed her desired course of action. The Princess of Wands is able to place herself at the centre of any activity and use it to fuel her own vigorous activity. She has a burning desire to achieve, and does so with brilliance and daring. At worst she is self-centred, theatrical and shallow in her interactions with others. She may spread her brilliance as energised enthusiasm through a group; alternatively she may sap the will of others to pursue her own selfish ends.

Personal development with the Princess of Wands card

The Princess of Wands counsels the individual to take opportunities as they are presented, but not to take advantage of others for self-aggrandisement.

The nature of the Princess shows the importance of keeping a determined purpose, so that eclecticism does not degenerate into an obsession with irrelevant detail. (This is evident in people whose aim of personal development is confused as they become engrossed in a mixture of tarot, runes, Jungian theory and Aztec symbolism – quite forgetting their original purpose.)

THE KNIGHT OF CUPS

Title:
The Lord of the Waves and the Waters; King of the Hosts of the Sea

Element: *Fire of Water*

The Knight is shown seated on a horse (in many packs, a winged horse) and carrying a chalice. The image is one of the motion and aggressive power of water. The crab and peacock are often depicted attending the Knight; they are emblems of the active, brilliant qualities of water.

The Knight represents the elastic nature of the unconscious, the way in which the deeper levels of the self hold innumerable currents which, at various times, surface in the conscious mind. He may be superficial, in the same way that dreams or other messages from the unconscious may be only shallow reflections of the mind's deeper activities. An important aspect of this card is shown by the interaction of Fire and Water: the motivating force of Fire moves Water, but the interaction of these Elements is not an easy one. The Knight is very susceptible to the forces within and around him. He is easily moved but less determined than his counterpart in the previous suit.

Personal development with the Knight of Cups card

This card shows the danger of becoming caught in the superficial aspects of the unconscious, of concentrating too much on the appearance of the message and missing its content. The reflective quality of this card shows the importance of attending to the tides within the unconscious mind and using these as springboards to other activity.

THE QUEEN OF CUPS

Title:
The Queen of the Thrones of Water

Element: *Water of Water*

Queen of Cups

The Queen is a most mysterious card. She is usually depicted as a woman holding a chalice and often with a water bird, such as an ibis, in attendance. Frequently the figure of the Queen is veiled or shrouded to such a degree that she is difficult to discern within the reflections of her watery environment.

The card represents the essential characteristics of the Water Element. The Queen is a shadowy figure. Little may be said about her character as she is a catalytic energy. She reflects and even distorts impressions that pass through her just as physical water reflects and refracts light.

The Queen of Cups is an emblem of passivity, patience and illusion. In one sense she is related to the way that impressions from the unconscious can emerge, sublimating the conscious mind and opening up the senses of clairvoyance. However, the illusion of this card shows that impressions may come either through the 'Gates of Ivory' or the 'Gates of Horn', i.e. coloured by the desires or activity of the individual ego, or more directly from the unconscious layers.

Personal development with the Queen of Cups card

The Queen of Cups counsels the importance of allowing the mind to become passive, in order to permit impressions and inspiration to well up from the unconscious levels. This is also a warning not to become enslaved in the net of illusions that the unconscious may generate. This card shows how passivity is the best means of transmission, for insight is most often gained by 'letting it come to you' rather than by trying to force the process.

Prince of Cups

THE PRINCE OF CUPS

Title:
The Prince of the Chariot of the Waters

Element: *Air of Water*

The figure in this card is usually shown dressed in armour and riding a chariot or horse through the air. The symbol of the eagle (which is associated with the astrological sign of Scorpio) may be depicted, along with the snake and scorpion. There is an aura of calm authority in this image and a sense that he hides great secrets.

The combination of the Elements of Air and Water naturally suggests rain or steam. In either case this card is concerned with the ability of water to change form, to move and to recombine in different ways and at different times. The Prince of Cups is a card of transmutation and transformation, closely related to Death in the Major Arcana. The process of putrefaction is also important in this symbol. The Prince represents the faculty of the mind that is able to take different elements, strip them down and use them as a fuel for its own purposes. The Prince will ruthlessly, determinedly seek to assure his own success. He is a character of subtle craft and skill; the spy, political candidate, diplomatic negotiator, seeker after occult wisdom.

Personal development with the Prince of Cups card

The Prince of Cups counsels the importance of stripping away old and outmoded ideas and of using the environment (both inner and outer) as a fuel with which to feed the process of self-understanding, integrating each experience into the aim of individuation. He suggests the development of a calm persona in situations where one might naturally allow emotions to be exposed. This card also shows how situations (such as memories of bad experiences) may be transmuted to provide fertile material from which self-understanding may grow.

THE PRINCESS OF CUPS

Title:
The Princess of the Waters
Element: *Earth of Water*

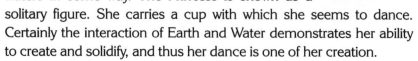

Often the background of this card shows the fertile earth or the bounty of the waters in some way. The Princess is shown as a solitary figure. She carries a cup with which she seems to dance. Certainly the interaction of Earth and Water demonstrates her ability to create and solidify, and thus her dance is one of her creation.

The ability to give substance and form to any idea is glyphed in this card. The Princess demonstrates the process by which ideas, emotions and indeed any activity of the mind is manifested. This card is that of the artist who is able to transmute a feeling from his or her own mind into the form of musical notes or painted canvas. It is also the ability of the inspired individual to express his or her understanding through teaching.

The Princess is able to crystallise an idea into reality, but first the other processes shown in the previous Water cards must have occurred (the Knight of Cups, motivation; Queen of Cups, acceptance; Prince of Cups, transmutation), leading, finally, to manifestation.

Personal development with the Princess of Cups card

The Princess demonstrates that the crystallisation of ideas is essential. If thoughts are not acted upon or actualised in any way then they become mere flights of fancy, escapist dreams without hope or intention of fulfilment. This card shows that the impressions from the unconscious must be applied and that, despite the passive action of water, it is vital to use insight gained in this way to 'open the lotus of understanding' rather than to let a flood of impressions obscure one's purpose.

Knight of Swords

THE KNIGHT OF SWORDS

Title:
The Lord of the Winds and Breezes; King of the Spirits of the Air

Element: *Fire of Air*

The central impression of this card, in all renderings of the tarot, is of swiftness. The Knight of Swords is often shown astride a horse which charges, sometimes literally, through the air. Birds such as swifts or swallows may be shown accompanying him. He holds his sword point forward, as though riding at breakneck speed into the fray.

The interaction between Fire and Air in this form is extremely powerful. Fire is will and drive, Air is intelligence and swiftness, thus the apparent breakneck ride of the Knight is not without planning or consideration. Unlike the Knight of Wands, the counterpart in the suit of Swords does not rely on valour alone to secure success. Instead, he acts swiftly but in accordance with a carefully arranged plan. Certainly this image is one of relentlessness, and although he may have planned his actions he may not have considered his underlying motivations very carefully.

Another point about this image is that it shows how, when energised, i.e. given direction by the Fire Element, the least substantial elemental force, Air, can become a storm capable of tearing down walls and lifting the waves into towering peaks.

Personal development with the Knight of Swords card

The Knight of Swords shows how intellectual ideas when fired by enthusiasm take on a great power. However, the individual must be careful not to become engulfed in this rush of activity. It is easy for what started out as the visionary aim of enlightening mankind to degenerate into a 'holy war against the unbelievers'. This shows the importance of continuously revising, renewing and analysing one's course of action, whatever it may be.

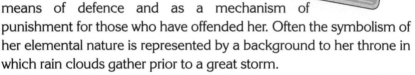

THE QUEEN OF SWORDS

Title:
The Queen of the Thrones of Air

Element: *Water of Air*

The Queen of Swords is often a stern image. She carries her swords both as a means of defence and as a mechanism of punishment for those who have offended her. Often the symbolism of her elemental nature is represented by a background to her throne in which rain clouds gather prior to a great storm.

This card is the emblem of the watcher, the individual who is able to stand a few steps back from the crowd and dispassionately observe the pageant of events around her. She is able to reconcile opposing views or situations, not by mediation but by distancing herself emotionally and intellectually from her surroundings. She is also reminiscent of Adjustment in the Major Arcana, a keeper of the balance between extremes but fierce in defending her own individuality and neutrality from bribery or direct attack.

When she does become involved in any situation, the Queen of Swords acts swiftly, asserting 'what is right', perhaps a painful process but one which, with her penetrating insight, she knows will bring the best results in the long term.

Personal development with the Queen of Swords card

The Queen of Swords counsels the individual to take the opportunity to stand apart from both his or her own emotions and those of others. By taking such a dispassionate stance a situation may be seen more clearly and a definite and correct choice of action taken. Yet there is also an injunction to remember that a coolly clinical attitude may be right for assessing a situation but is rarely good for dealing with one.

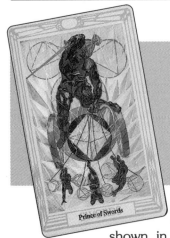

THE PRINCE OF SWORDS

Title:
The Prince of the Chariots of the Winds

Element: *Air of Air*

The picture on this card is again one of speed and swiftness. The Prince may be shown in a chariot, sometimes being pulled by winged figures that appear to dart around the sky as they draw the chariot after them. The Prince raises his sword aloft, ready to strike at whatever lies before him.

There is no stability, no settlement and little in the way of defined purpose in this card. The intellectual nature of the Air Element shows the Prince continually generating, analysing and destroying thoughts, none of which is seen through into any form of application.

The Prince of Swords is totally flexible, able to move through innumerable different beliefs, arguments and situations. He holds each steadfastly but only for a brief period of time before his restless and unstable nature drives him on, perhaps to take a position directly contrary to the one he held five minutes before! The logical process shown in this card operates at a totally abstract level but requires the interaction of other forces if the ideas developed are to come to fruition.

Personal development with the Prince of Swords card

The Prince of Swords shows that, at times, an intensely analytical frame of mind should be adopted. Logic and reason should be allowed to scrutinise every aspect of the individual's personal development. If this process is carried to extremes it will provide little insight and still less counsel for future action, but logic and intellectual capabilities are excellent if applied in the right way and direction. However, the unconscious will never give up its secrets to the rational mind and it is important to recognise this limitation.

THE PRINCESS OF SWORDS

Title:
*The Princess of the Rushing Winds;
Lotus of the Palace of Air*

Element: *Earth of Air*

Princess of Swords

The Princess of Swords is an aggressive figure. She may be shown brandishing her sword, perhaps with the dismembered body of her foe at her feet. Storm clouds gather around her. The whole feel of the card is one of militant power and strength.

The figure in this card is the angel of deliverance for some and the force of retribution for others. She is a skilled negotiator, able to discern the practicalities of the most complex situation. (As her mother the Queen deals with emotions, so the Princess deals with their earthly counterparts: actions and practicalities.)

The Princess of Swords is able to deal with the disputes of others but is little prepared to apply her analytical spirit to herself. She may try to set others around her, even the whole world, to rights, but ignore the faults in herself.

An important feature of this symbol is the impetus to act. She is especially concerned with setting limitations to action and in this way is related to the much misunderstood force of karma or the principle of action and reaction.

Personal development with the Princess of Swords card

The Princess of Swords shows the importance of applying one's judgement, and not just to others but to oneself also. She shows that the Air Element, logic and reason, has limitations.

This Princess is concerned with the importance of application. Just as the Princess of Cups asserts the importance of applying one's intuition, so the Princess of Swords suggests that rational thought is pointless unless manifest in some way. She is further concerned with the abilities of discrimination and evaluation, for if ideas do not bear fruit she cuts them down.

Knight of Disks

THE KNIGHT OF DISCS

Title:
The Lord of the Wild and Fertile Land; King of the Spirits of Earth

Element: *Fire of Earth*

The Knight of Discs is seated firmly on his horse, which is frequently a warhorse or another large-limbed animal. His disc is a shield but it seems to have little defensive purpose and is more of a heraldic device. The countryside around him is usually shown as being ripe for harvest.

The Knight of Discs is very much 'the natural'; he may not display great intellectual prowess but he is greatly skilled in the application of his instinct. He may be the blacksmith, the carver, the farmer, or the skilled craftsman who is able to put his mark on nature not by dominating it but by allowing his own 'inner nature' to bloom.

The Knight may seem slow-witted and dull in comparison to his counterparts in the suits of Wands, Cups and Swords. Yet the force of Fire has been harnessed within him. He is the fire of growth, the drive of nature to create and destroy and re-create anew.

Personal development with the Knight of Discs card
The Knight of Discs counsels the individual to learn to appreciate the process of growth, to delight in the slow but majestic development of the oak tree as much as in the swift but ephemeral sparks of the firecracker. There is also a suggestion that 'getting back to the soil' or discovering one's racial or ethnic roots can be a source of empowerment and may permit the individual to see him or herself as part of a greater continuum of creation.

THE QUEEN OF DISCS

Title:
The Queen of the Thrones of Earth
Element: *Water of Earth*

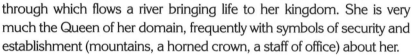

Queen of Disks

The interaction of Water and Earth results in fertility. As such, the Queen of Discs may be depicted against a background of countryside through which flows a river bringing life to her kingdom. She is very much the Queen of her domain, frequently with symbols of security and establishment (mountains, a horned crown, a staff of office) about her.

The Queen of Discs represents the pulsating rhythm of life that nurtures the earth. She is selfless and steadfast in protecting her own and will do her utmost to turn any influence that mars her creative ability. In the parlance of modern ecological thought, she is the image of Gaia, the self-regulating, changing yet stable system of interlocking species on our planet.

As she is physical fertility she is also fertility at other levels. She is the motivating force within the psyche that brings fresh ideas and sees them translated into actuality. It is interesting to note that, being as she is a figure representing wild nature or wilderness, many great human insights have come when human beings make direct contact with the natural world (Leonardo's inspiration for inventions from observing animals, the Buddha's enlightenment under a tree, Christ's revelations in the wilderness).

Personal development with the Queen of Discs card

The Queen of Discs shows that insight may be a gradual process, having different seasons but always continuing. She suggests that the most profound understanding of the unconscious, indeed the whole of the self, may be had from experiencing the interplay of complex forces that make up the natural world. In one sense she is an affirmation of the microcosm/macrocosm principle, i.e. that the universe outside the individual is a direct reflection of the individual's own inner nature.

THE PRINCE OF DISCS

Title:
The Prince of the Chariot of Earth

Element: *Air of Earth*

The Prince may be shown seated in a chariot, often pulled by an animal symbolic of Earth (such as an ox). He is a stable figure, solid and meditative. He is quiet, as if absorbed in some careful planning, using the intellect of Air in a harmonious and careful way.

The Prince of Discs is a manager. Unlike his counterpart in the Swords suit, he carefully applies his intelligence to the matter and facilities at his disposal in order to create the right effect.

This card represents one of the most remarkable features of humanity – our great ingenuity. But he knows that however he acts there are many factors to take into consideration. His action is not for short-term gain but has a greater design, so he works in accordance with the forces around him, benefiting from such alliances and not seeing them as a threat or opposition to his own design.

His insight and reason are so penetrating that he can see the worth in all things, though if he takes this to excess it could indicate a rapacious materialism.

Personal development with the Prince of Discs card

This card shows how logical processes must be made to work in harmony with the forces of nature. The aim of personal development or individuation is not for the rational mind to have dominion over the unconscious but instead to work in partnership with it. The good farmer does not dominate or subdue his land but works his or her own will in accordance with nature's laws and thereby gains the greatest and most valuable yield.

THE PRINCESS OF DISCS

Title:
The Princess of the Echoing Hills;
Rose of the Palaces of Earth

Element: *Earth of Earth*

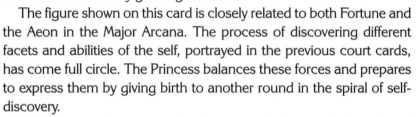

Princess of Disks

There is a brooding sense of creation about to occur in this, the last of the court cards. Like the Queen of Discs, the Princess is frequently shown with mountains and horns, representing her power in the sphere of manifestation. Some decks show her pregnant, the seed of creative ability growing within her.

The figure shown on this card is closely related to both Fortune and the Aeon in the Major Arcana. The process of discovering different facets and abilities of the self, portrayed in the previous court cards, has come full circle. The Princess balances these forces and prepares to express them by giving birth to another round in the spiral of self-discovery.

Meditation on the events that have gone before is the function of this card. She integrates and invigorates the past, yet there is something of the 'random factor' in the process for it is impossible to tell just how the next phase will develop.

The Princess carries with her the legacy of the past and the infinite potentials of the future. She is the vehicle of continuous growth.

Personal development with the Princess of Discs card

The Princess of Discs counsels the individual to turn inward, to meditate on what has happened before and, simultaneously, to look to the future. She serves to remind the individual that nothing can ever be known for certain. One may be sure only of the 'now', for both past and future are ghosts (especially since the unconscious does not seem to perceive time as consciousness does). The only reality, if there is such a thing, is 'now', a point in time from which anything can happen and which is the result of infinite factors. Learning to see oneself as, simultaneously, the least important and also the greatest of the universe's children is the lesson of this card.

THE ACE OF WANDS

Title:
The Root of the Power of Fire

Element: *Fire*

The 'Wand' usually appears as a single rod, often a club, rudely carved and held vertically. It is a symbol of great power, potency and authority.

This card represents Fire in its purest, simplest and most unstable form. The Ace of Wands is the root driving force of all action. In the psyche of the individual it is concerned with the basic drive of the will, which must be carefully focused and directed if it is to have proper effect. New beginnings, ideas and changes are motivated by this force. The Fire of the Ace of Wands is an unstable power. Like physical fire, it must be treated with respect; it requires careful handling if it is to be productive rather than detrimental or dissipated in wasteful frustration.

This is the power that drives the stars as much as it is the driving force in the self. It is raw energy, boundless and unlimited.

Personal development with the Ace of Wands card

The Ace of Wands shows that the will of the individual is an immeasurable, powerful force. However, this blind force requires understanding before it may be applied appropriately. The symbol is one of great potential but it is totally ambivalent. It may be the drive that goads the scientist to a new discovery, or the despot to seek the position of tyrant, or the healer to find a successful cure. Fire, real or symbolic, must be respected and handled with care.

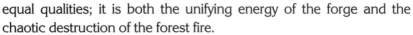

THE TWO OF WANDS

Title:
The Lord of Dominion

Element: *Fire*

Many decks show the two wands in this image crossed over each other. Certainly the implication is a reaffirmation that Fire has two equal qualities; it is both the unifying energy of the forge and the chaotic destruction of the forest fire.

The word 'dominion' of this card's title means a sphere of influence. In this symbol the dual nature of Fire is expressed, as is the dominating quality of its action. This is a card of power – power by restriction and conservation. As with all the cards, this force has two sides, being essentially amoral in itself. The restraint may be that which spurs a pressure group to defend a beautiful woodland, or which binds their action with the legally enforceable red tape of bureaucracy.

An important symbolic meaning of this card is that destruction is always the first part of the creative process. The one wand becomes two, splitting apart the blind power of Fire into opposites which may then interact.

Personal development with the Two of Wands card

The Two of Wands recalls the fact that division is necessary before cohesion can be accomplished. One of the saddest features of modern society is that a nation becomes cohesive and 'pulls together' only when in opposition to another nation. The Two shows how understanding, action and change can occur only when an established state is destroyed. Thus in reproduction the sperm cell and ovum must lose their distinct identity for fertilisation to take place. We establish relationships with others, especially our parents, but we must be ready to split apart from the parental unit in order to establish a separate but related identity.

THE THREE OF WANDS

Title:
The Lord of Established Strength
Element: *Fire*

The three wands in this card are often shown in a triangular formation. The triangle is important in that it is the geometric figure, enclosing an area within it, comprised of the least number of straight lines. The three-dimensional form of the triangle is the tetrahedron. Apart from the sphere, this is the simplest three-dimensional form and has four triangular faces. As it is the form with the least volume to surface area, it can withstand the greatest amount of external pressure – it is the strongest shape. This fits well with the title of 'Established Strength'.

In this card the energy of the Ace of Wands, which received its 'initial break' in the Two, prepares to come into manifestation. This is the point in the process of manifestation where the first buds appear. These may herald the successful initiation of a new project, venture or explorative process within the self. However, there is an injunction to continue and not to be lulled into a false sense of security in which the conscious mind might mistake the blossom on the tree as a sure sign that the fruit of success is assured without further effort.

Personal development with the Three of Wands card

The Three of Wands is concerned with beginnings which, even if they seem certainly established, are delicate things. The message from this card is not to congratulate oneself too much about the success of any initial phase of an undertaking while forgetting to pursue the next stages necessary.

This card also affirms that before any act of creation can occur a solid basis is required for it to grow. In other words, the Three reminds us that a firm foundation is as necessary for self-exploration as it is for building a house.

THE FOUR OF WANDS

Title:
The Lord of Perfected Work

Element: *Fire*

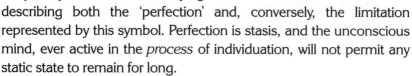

The wands in this card are often shown crossed to form a wheel of eight points. They may well be shown lying within a circle, describing both the 'perfection' and, conversely, the limitation represented by this symbol. Perfection is stasis, and the unconscious mind, ever active in the *process* of individuation, will not permit any static state to remain for long.

In this card the Fire of the Ace has become transformed into an established order; one might think of the Four of Wands as the emblem of a society that, superficially, appears settled and tranquil.

Part of the symbolism of this card is the affirmation that the work initiated by Fire cannot be fulfilled unless tact and gentleness are used as well as force and vigour.

Personal development with the Four of Wands card

In a sense this card represents the quiet before the storm and is an injunction to the individual to learn what may be learned from peace and stability but (as with the Tower of the Major Arcana) not let comfort become a hindrance for further development. This card also demonstrates the way that, when governed correctly, the fiery aspects of the psyche can have a gentle rather than an aggressive action. An instance of this may be seen in medicine where a gentle warmth is used to relieve pain.

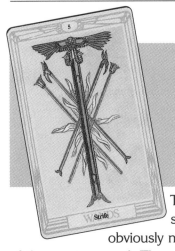

THE FIVE OF WANDS

Title:
The Lord of Strife

Element: *Fire*

The five wands in this card are often shown with the fifth wand larger and obviously more dominant than in the peaceful four of the previous card. The overall aura of this card appears not just gloomy but positively violent.

This card is like a volcano. It is the image of Fire which, though repressed, breeds itself into violent action, destroying established structures but also throwing up fertilising material that can form the basis of new growth. This card has a heavy feminine influence. It is the phoenix, which dies through fire in order to be reborn. This metaphor of rebirth through the fiery, feminine energies of the psyche is of great importance. Although one may tend to think of Fire as a masculine energy, its greatest force is feminine in expression. In this card we see the dual aspects of Mother Nature, both beautiful and terrible. She destroys the apparent perfection, roses wither and the land is thrown into turmoil by her volcanic power.

Personal development with the Five of Wands card

Periodically the unconscious mind re-creates such a volcano in the human psyche. It throws the conscious mind into total disarray. However, it also lays down a fertile soil in which new understanding may develop. The individual must learn to appreciate this force and, vitally, not fight against it. Personal development is a beneficial process, but it is not a painless one.

THE SIX OF WANDS

Title:
The Lord of Victory

Element: *Fire*

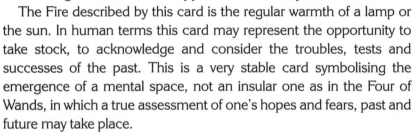

The Six of Wands is a light and beneficent card after the violent action of the Five. Often the sun is shown in the rendition, shining and illuminating the wands which appear harmoniously interlinked.

The Fire described by this card is the regular warmth of a lamp or the sun. In human terms this card may represent the opportunity to take stock, to acknowledge and consider the troubles, tests and successes of the past. This is a very stable card symbolising the emergence of a mental space, not an insular one as in the Four of Wands, in which a true assessment of one's hopes and fears, past and future may take place.

The steady, though open, structure glyphed by this card also permits the past and wished-for future to be put into context. However, the sunshine of this card can degenerate into periods of inactivity and bathing in the reflected glory of one's past successes.

Personal development with the Six of Wands card

The Six of Wands counsels the individual to make an opportunity to take stock of the present, to see that one's present situation is informed by the past and connected to the future.

This card symbolises a period of rest in which one's personal development may be appreciated in a greater context. The path to individuation is as relevant to others as it is to the individual who actively pursues this course. It is important to bear in mind how one's own development affects other people. You will see how a change in the self is often reflected in other people, whose attitude and behaviour towards you similarly change.

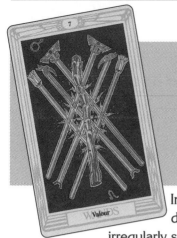

THE SEVEN OF WANDS

Title:
The Lord of Valour

Element: *Fire*

In this card the image is of six wands dominated by a seventh, usually an irregularly shaped club or staff. There is a feeling of confrontation and something of a lack of predetermined purpose in this card.

In the Seven of Wands the unity of the Six has broken down. The force of the Fire Element goes in all directions without any systematic purpose. The wand that has been added to the union of the Six is a rude club which shows that the only direction inherent in the card exists in the most basic form. The title 'Lord of Valour' further suggests that success using this card's energy is not to be gained by planning or foresight; instead, what is needed is raw individual courage to bring about a successful conclusion.

The Fire in the Seven of Wands is riotous and irrational. Just like the unconscious forces in humanity, it has a potential for massive creativity or rampant and pointless destruction.

Personal development with the Seven of Wands card

The Seven of Wands shows that there are certain situations in which logical, conscious planning is ineffective. Instead, the psyche must trust in the basic impulse to succeed, and triumph by dint of the individual spirit. By abandoning the rational method the mind may unleash reserves of creativity, ingenuity or determination that would otherwise remain hidden. The symbol also suggests that in a complex situation sometimes the unconscious forces provide the best allies; instances where acts of individual valour, spurred on by something other than conscious reasoning, have succeeded where all else fails fill the history books.

THE EIGHT OF WANDS

Title:
The Lord of Swiftness

Element: *Fire*

In this card the restless wands of the Seven have become ordered once again. Often the wands are shown rayed out or flying through the air. In most renditions the flames of fire have disappeared, to be replaced by a fine electrical brilliance.

This is a card of communication *par excellence.* The Fire of the Wands suit has become the electrical 'fire' which sends messages in the body, animating the brain and speech. In the modern era of information technology the relationship between the electrical 'fire' of this card and contemporary communication systems is apparent.

The wands show connections being swiftly made to all parts of the universe (inner and outer). This card also shows how subtle energies are the underlying feature of the universe and recall the axiom that 'everything is energy' and can be communicated with.

There is also a hint of trickery in this card, as this goes hand in hand with the ability to communicate. To speak implies the ability to remain silent, to bend words, to imply subtle shades of meaning, and to lie.

Personal development with the Eight of Wands card

The Eight of Wands demonstrates the importance of communication, of developing this skill in relation to *everything* in the universe. It is good to open the channels of communication within regions of the self, but one's skills should be cultivated in other areas as well. There is no use in being able to talk to an archetype and not to one's lover!

An important lesson in this card is that communication combines a delicate mix of reaching out and remaining open to incoming communications. We often say 'talking' is a communication form, but it is only as effective as our ability to listen.

THE NINE OF WANDS

Title:
The Lord of Strength

Element: *Fire*

The overall feeling of this card is one of establishment. The force of Fire has become not only manifest but also rooted firmly in the earth. Some decks portray this graphically by showing the nine wands planted firmly in the earth and showing the beginnings of shoots forming upon them.

This card is very much concerned with the innate Fire in nature, the forces of birth, growth, death and decay. The image in this card is very much one of health and vitality. As in the Four and Six, this card shows the establishment of a complete system. The system remains constant by virtue of its ability to change, to move from one stable state to another.

A sense of enormous productivity attends this symbol, with a recognition that 'change is stability'. Much more can be achieved when, instead of being limited to linear concepts, seeing the universe as a refining process from worst to better to best, each point in the cycle of change is valued in itself.

Personal development with the Nine of Wands card

The Nine of Wands counsels the individual to discover what innate strengths exist within the self. It asserts the importance of examining the features of the psyche and of applying such insight in a practical way to benefit the work of individuation.

There is also an injunction to beware of obstinacy in this card; one is reminded of King Canute, his consciousness at odds with unconscious knowledge, vainly railing against the oncoming tide.

THE TEN OF WANDS

Title:
The Lord of Oppression

Element: *Fire*

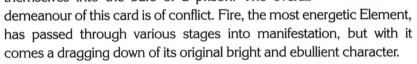

In this card the wands of the Nine are added to and we see them form themselves into the bars of a prison. The overall demeanour of this card is of conflict. Fire, the most energetic Element, has passed through various stages into manifestation, but with it comes a dragging down of its original bright and ebullient character.

As the last card in the suit of Wands this symbol represents the price of success. The Element of Fire can go no further without being unified with the other elemental forces. The notion of responsibility is of vital importance in this card. Responsibility is something that should be earned, but when it comes unbidden or without understanding it represses and constrains action. With the establishment of a new order, or an increased awareness, comes the responsibility of maintaining the territory; this is as true of an army that conquers a new land as it is for the individual who has arrived at a particular basis of understanding through personal development. The fiery force must give up control to the interaction of other aspects of the elemental system or it will become trapped.

Personal development with the Ten of Wands card

This card acknowledges the necessity of combining other elemental forces in the task of personal development if that process is to be pursued successfully. It also reminds the individual that knowledge brings with it the responsibility to use it wisely.

Finally, the Ten of Wands is a reminder that it is possible to backslide and lose ground as a result of internal or external factors. It is therefore suggested that the individual should periodically reassess his or her success or moral attitudes and ensure that the consciousness is not saying one thing while the ego does another!

THE ACE OF CUPS

Title:
The Root of the Power of Water
Element: *Water*

In this card a large chalice is shown, often with a dove or white light descending on to the vessel. The cup seems full of a liquid which is as much a light as it is a fluid. Often the sea or reflections of water are used as the background to this image.

The Ace of Cups represents the Element of Water in its primordial form. Water is very much the emblem of the unconscious. In Christian myth the spirit of God moves over the impenetrable depths of the waters before creating life and, subsequently, Adam.

The Cup represents the womb from which all creation issues. Yet in the Act the force of water has yet to be reacted upon by outside forces. There is an abundance of potential but the way that potential will formulate itself is not decided in this symbol. As an image of the unconscious, the Ace of Cups shows the necessity for the evolution of consciousness, for it is only by the dynamic interplay of these two forces that the process of individuation can occur.

Personal development with the Ace of Cups card

As the unconscious level informs the conscious mind of the individual so the conscious mind may plant a seed in the unconscious layer. The Ace of Cups demonstrates that the unconscious must interact with the conscious before it can create. This card shows a period in which great potential exists but no direction or fertilisation is yet apparent. If the seeds of wisdom sown are the sound seeds of personal discovery then the harvest will be rewarding and fulfilling.

THE TWO OF CUPS

Title:
The Lord of Love

Element: *Water*

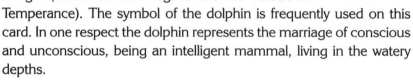

In this card the two chalices are often seen exchanging water in the form of rays of light (similar to the image of the two vessels in Temperance). The symbol of the dolphin is frequently used on this card. In one respect the dolphin represents the marriage of conscious and unconscious, being an intelligent mammal, living in the watery depths.

The dolphin is an important alchemical symbol; it represents 'Royal Art', that is, the combination of duality into unity. Love, in the sense of this card, represents unity formed by the mutual annihilation of opposites; by this process a new situation is created.

The alchemical process represented in this symbol is akin to the 'sacred marriage' in the Lovers and Temperance of the Major Arcana. Psychologically, it is this 'love' that is the emotional impetus for personal development. The conscious and unconscious minds are separated but, when they touch, they generate the ego. While the ego is often railed against for being an adversary to personal development, it is the seed which, carefully tended, will mature to form a whole individual.

Personal development with the Two of Cups card

The Two of Cups shows the importance of unifying any divided elements in the human psyche. This process does not lead to an abandonment of conscious awareness or of sublimation of the persona: it is more a question of making certain that the psyche is not divided against itself. Discovering the developing nature of the self is virtually impossible if the individual is conducting a civil war within his or her own mind.

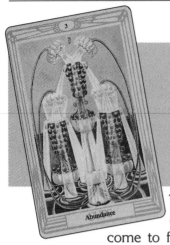

THE THREE OF CUPS

Title:
The Lord of Abundance

Element: *Water*

This card typically shows three cups about which are the emblems of fertility come to fruition. Fruits, especially pomegranates, are often included and the triad of cups appear filled with bright water.

The Three of Cups represents the emergence of the 'third thing' hinted at in the Two of Cups. In this symbol Water's creativity is shown – the bounty of the Water of the unconscious, which, when the ego permits, brings forth dreams, visions, inspiration and fresh awareness. This release of hidden potential is a great vitalising force for the conscious mind, bringing a sensation of joy and celebration. This can occur when, suddenly, the unconscious provides a new way of seeing or of appreciating the universe at either inner or outer levels.

Implicit in this image is also a hint that abundance can lead to self-satisfaction and that such an insight may be viewed as a goal in itself rather than a prompt to deeper investigation and application.

Personal development with the Three of Cups card

The Three of Cups heralds the emergence of new, hidden and even mysterious messages from the unconscious layers. It may also relate to periods when one seems to 'see clearly' as if experiencing the world for the first time. This harvest of inspiration and fertility of mind should not remain unquestioned; as Water is also the Element of illusion, it is important that the analytical and even conservative functions of the conscious are brought to bear on these matters.

THE FOUR OF CUPS

Title:
The Lord of Blended Pleasure

Element: *Water*

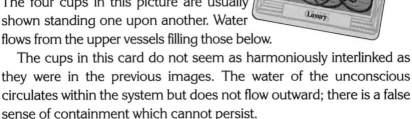

The four cups in this picture are usually shown standing one upon another. Water flows from the upper vessels filling those below.

The cups in this card do not seem as harmoniously interlinked as they were in the previous images. The water of the unconscious circulates within the system but does not flow outward; there is a false sense of containment which cannot persist.

This is a symbol of water harnessed – either physical water dammed up and generating power, or the ocean of the unconscious harnessed to do a specific task. The problem here is that inspiration from the unconscious is capricious and works best when unlooked for. By attempting to control the power of Water, dissatisfaction results.

Personal development with the Four of Cups card

The Four of Cups marks a time of re-evaluation in the face of increasingly satiated and static existence. The emotional qualities of the Water/unconscious force must be allowed to find their own direction and level. In one sense the original inspiration has degenerated; the artist from whom society demands a continual output of repetitive work turns into a hack. The card also suggests that the individual should focus attention on the ego, which can act either as a sluice gate for unconscious information or as a censorious force that splits the productive interaction shown in the Two of Cups.

THE FIVE OF CUPS

Title:
The Lord of Loss in Pleasure

Element: *Water*

In this card the five cups are shown split or empty. The sense of this card is one of sorrow but not of outright loss. Any flowers that are shown appear to lose their petals and the whole scene is one of aridity and disturbance.

In this card the Water Element has begun to dry up and pass into the skies. This is an image of the first stages of decay where trouble is stirred up and structures are destroyed. The Five of Cups is loss and disruption where conflicting forces battle.

In a beneficial sense the pedestrian and humdrum system of the Four of Cups is brought down but there is a necessary period of stillness before new activity can commence.

It may seem that circumstances conspire to thwart the best laid plans. Yet even failure is itself a result and, when seen overall, just as enlightening as rapturous success.

Personal development with the Five of Cups card
The Five of Cups is a trough in the progress of the Water Element's activity. It is a time where everything seems frustrated and futile; the cups are empty of all input. After the experience of any great loss, one eventually feels empty of emotions, as though they have been used up and spent. A corresponding situation is that of an empty cup which can only be filled. The individual should bide his or her time until a broader horizon presents itself.

THE SIX OF CUPS

Title:
The Lord of Pleasure
Element: *Water*

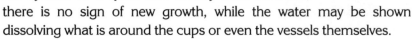

In this card a more balanced scheme of the cups is shown. Water flows through the system at a quiet and orderly rate. However, there is no sign of new growth, while the water may be shown dissolving what is around the cups or even the vessels themselves.

The process of disintegration begun violently in the Five is continued here but at a more regular pace. A feature of the Element of Water is its ability to dissolve; this applies as much to the elements in the psyche as it does to salt in physical water. In this card the disintegration process permits hidden levels of the psyche to be discovered and secret parts of the self to be illuminated. The concept of understanding is also related to the Element of Water. Here understanding dawns as the individual's past and present state of mind is accessed and reintegration begins. However, this introversion may imply a nostalgic narcissism if unlocked portions of one's inner nature are not examined in new ways.

Personal development with the Six of Cups card

This card heralds a gradual and gentle breaking down of barriers within the psyche. It enjoins the individual to look for new ways in which the emotional content of the mind may be viewed. It also describes the purifying aspect of Water, which is able to wash away the stains of guilt, fear and loss, not by asserting the rational but by permitting these emotions to be experienced to the full and dealt with in a constructive way.

THE SEVEN OF CUPS

Title:
The Lord of Illusionary Success

Element: *Water*

In many decks the seven cups in this image are shown with various images upon them, representing many possibilities. The cards may appear somewhat distant or abstracted from the usual course of things.

This is a card of confusion, confounding the individual with the innumerable avenues that were opened up in the Six. The confusion felt in this card can come about in any number of ways. In this card the unconscious sets forth an emotional drive that the conscious cannot understand or put into context – the person feels something but has no inkling of what it is.

The element of illusion present in this card represents a very difficult situation. Conscious logic is required to direct emotional responses and to become aware of them; however too much logic throttles emotionality. The difficulty here is finding a middle way where one is trapped neither in the idle dream of Water nor in the bland logic of robotic existence.

Personal development with the Seven of Cups card

This card shows that logical thought can be the partner of emotionality and intuition. The Seven of Cups reveals numerous directions of action, but if this is not to result in a painful, drawn-out quandary, the careful guidance of logic is required. Impressions from the unconscious should be qualified by the conscious mind but be neither subdued nor ignored.

This card also warns against trying to follow many roads in a half-hearted way rather than making a determined choice.

THE EIGHT OF CUPS

Title:
The Lord of Abandoned Success
Element: *Water*

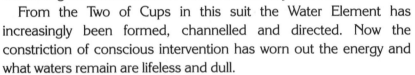

In this card the Water Element seems completely stagnant. There is no movement perceptible either at its surface or beneath the waves. The cups seem old and broken, incapable of containing the Water/unconscious forces as they once did.

From the Two of Cups in this suit the Water Element has increasingly been formed, channelled and directed. Now the constriction of conscious intervention has worn out the energy and what waters remain are lifeless and dull.

Considered psychologically, this process refers to a period in which the psyche seems hopelessly run down. No new inspiration or recharging of the emotional batteries takes place. The only option is to permit emotions and visions to go, for, like physical water, they require periodic revitalisation by aeration. This is a card of letting go, both of emotional constraints and of emotions themselves.

Personal development with the Eight of Cups card

The Eight of Cups suggests the importance of allowing to disperse whatever visions or emotions the consciousness clings to. By allowing feelings to slip into the background, and by opening up the psyche to new impressions, in time they will re-emerge. In the meantime, the individual should look to the conscious mind and prepare new vessels – belief systems, attitudes and exercises – into which the revitalised current of watery insight may flow.

THE NINE OF CUPS

Title:
The Lord of Material Happiness
Element: *Water*

In this card the cups are often shown as filled with brilliant white water, reminiscent of that filling the Ace of Cups. The sense of the card is one of lightness, brightness and renewal.

This is a card of renewal and revitalisation. In it the watery forces that seemed to desert the individual in the Eight return and are made manifest. This may refer to the final birth of the seed planted in the Ace and activated in the Two. In this card a dynamic equilibrium has been forged between the conscious and unconscious minds, with emotions and experiences informing both but threatening the integrity of neither level.

Ideally, a cycle should exist in the individual where emotions well up in the unconscious and are qualified by the conscious. They are then fed back into the unconscious layer to develop and bloom in the form of an increased understanding of the self.

Personal development with the Nine of Cups card

This card is concerned with seeing holistically and creating a situation where periods of relaxation and activity permit a regular flow of information through both conscious and unconscious minds. The card also shows the unifying force of Water as seen in group emotionality, and even in the visionary attitude of some religious organisations. Finally there is an injunction to manifest one's emotional and intuitive understanding in an outward form, to apply it to all levels of one's existence.

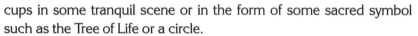

THE TEN OF CUPS

Title:
The Lord of Perfected Success
Element: *Water*

There are diverse representations of this card, but most often the 'success' mentioned in the title is shown by displaying the cups in some tranquil scene or in the form of some sacred symbol such as the Tree of Life or a circle.

This card has a relaxed atmosphere. Nevertheless, there is development, a process going on but, as with the Six of Cups, it is gradual and gentle. This card shows the dissolution of Water and marks the transition of the Water Element into Air – the Element of the following suit of Swords.

Connection with the watery unconscious nature demands the correct use of intelligence to balance this input into the conscious mind. Yet it is necessary for emotion to temper logic, and in the final analysis the emotional connection is the most important. An excellent instance of this idea comes from the native North American peoples who would castigate a fellow member of their tribe by saying 'you think with your head', implying that intuition and emotion had become dominated by shallow, ego-centred reason.

Personal development with the Ten of Cups card
This card glyphs the necessity of moving one's attention from the emotional unconscious into dealing with the logical conscious mind. There needs now to be a shift in emphasis. Whereas one's intelligence was used to keep intuition under control, now emotions must be called upon to give direction and warmth to the intellect.

THE ACE OF SWORDS

Title:
The Root of the Power of Air

Element: *Air*

This card generally depicts a double-edged broadsword held point upwards. Frequently a royal crown is shown encircling the blade. The image is one of power but is less violent in its nature than the Ace of Wands.

Air is the Element of the mental process and the Ace of Swords represents this aspect of the self in its embryonic form. With this Element the process within each Sword card, and the suit as a whole, is one of analysis, experiment and theorisation.

When humans use the logical process to understand anything, the first action is to analyse, to divide (hence the symbol of the sword) the problem into various elements, e.g. subject/object, organic/inorganic, long-term/short-term, etc. The process of experimentation then provides further data which, in time, may lead to a theory or an intellectual, abstract idea of how the world works, e.g. $E = MC^2$. The Ace of Swords shows the basis of this process, the drive of the individual to know, to understand and also to communicate intellectually as well as emotionally with the outer and inner universe.

Personal development with the Ace of Swords card

The Ace of Swords represents not only the intellectual drive to understand but also the unconscious drive towards individuation. The process of becoming a true individual, literally 'not divided', necessitates the ability of the mind to discriminate, to communicate, to appreciate and finally to reconcile those features in the universe that may appear as opposites.

THE TWO OF SWORDS

Title:
The Lord of Peace Restored
Element: *Air*

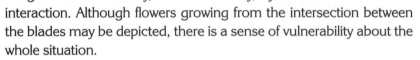

In this card the two swords are most often shown with their blades crossed. The image is one of stability, but not an easy, dynamic interaction. Although flowers growing from the intersection between the blades may be depicted, there is a sense of vulnerability about the whole situation.

In this card the thinking process of Air has begun. The motivation of the Ace resolves itself in the first action of the thought process – analysis. The two swords show the universe being divided into duality, thesis and antithesis, negative and positive. There is a definite sense of harmony in this card. While opposite ideas exist they do so in one image and both may be seen as valuable but in different ways. This is a symbol of intellectual reconciliation, yet thought still exists at an abstract level in this card; there is no application of the ideas generated.

Personal development with the Two of Swords card

The Two of Swords shows how ideas that may appear to be mutually exclusive are actually aspects of the same thing: for instance light and dark are considered opposites, though light exists only because darkness does and vice versa. This card further shows the importance of deciding on an intellectual course, of following the investigative process and of applying the intellect to levels other than the pure abstract. In other words, there is a warning against 'armchair intellectualism', which may evolve brilliant ideas but nothing of applicable worth.

THE THREE OF SWORDS

Title:
The Lord of Sorrow

Element: *Air*

In this card the three swords interact violently; the third sword shatters the union of the Two. Storm clouds or a darkened sky are usually shown in the background of this image.

In the Three of Swords the aloof abstraction of the Two breaks down. The original system has been thrown into chaos with one's intellectual view of the universe unable to be reconciled with the way in which the universe actually appears to work. This discrepancy is observable in many belief systems, religions and philosophies. While the mind holds that one set of ideas is 'moral', 'right' or 'normal', nature does not follow the order that the belief system would impose on it.

One beneficial aspect of this process is that 'out of chaos comes forth order' – from the confused maelstrom of thought new ideas are born. These may either be abortive attempts to patch up one's own belief system in the face of opposing information, or new insights into the nature of existence.

Personal development with the Three of Swords card

The Three of Swords advises against maintaining one's belief in the face of a changing understanding, where the facts that the individual would like to be true are no longer relevant. This symbol also shows that, from the disorder that comes when one's belief system is shaken, new ideas can be born. Co-operation and investigation of that which may appear opposed to one's own views can provide new insight. New experience must be gained, and teaching or listening to the converted is to be avoided.

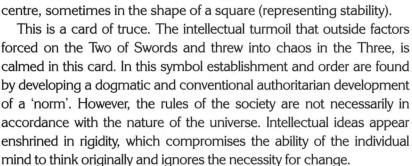

THE FOUR OF SWORDS

Title:
The Lord of Rest from Strife

Element: *Air*

In this symbol the four swords are shown redeeming the chaos of the Three of Swords. The swords are often shown in a regular formation, with their points touching, sometimes directed to one centre, sometimes in the shape of a square (representing stability).

This is a card of truce. The intellectual turmoil that outside factors forced on the Two of Swords and threw into chaos in the Three, is calmed in this card. In this symbol establishment and order are found by developing a dogmatic and conventional authoritarian development of a 'norm'. However, the rules of the society are not necessarily in accordance with the nature of the universe. Intellectual ideas appear enshrined in rigidity, which compromises the ability of the individual mind to think originally and ignores the necessity for change.

This process is useful if one is able to step away from it, and view 'normality' as an arbitrary quality rather than a universal one.

Personal development with the Four of Swords card
This card counsels the individual to avoid becoming trapped in any dogmatic belief structure, be it a religion, a political idea or a moral judgement. It suggests that such systems are useful when viewed together and similarities or dissimilarities teased out. Comparative mythology is one way in which this may be done, as it liberates the central core of human thought from its cultural basis. The Four shows that subscribing to a belief system can be productive only if one acknowledges the possibility of changing one's views, either within the system or by adopting a new one.

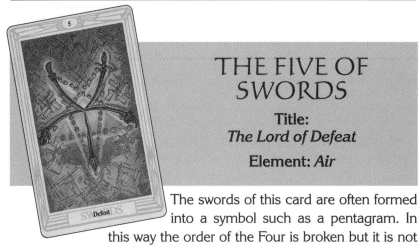

THE FIVE OF SWORDS

Title:
The Lord of Defeat

Element: *Air*

The swords of this card are often formed into a symbol such as a pentagram. In this way the order of the Four is broken but it is not violently smashed. Instead, the Four is 'overbalanced' and the dogma of that card weakened.

The motivation to understand, which leads to the development of a 'law' in the previous card, returns in the Five of Swords. In this symbol gaps and errors in the conventionality of the Four are discovered and exploited. The 'normality' that the Four enshrined breaks down, falling in on itself. By breaking down the barriers of the Four this card provides excellent opportunities for extending one's knowledge. Communication can be established with others, new experiences gained and a richer understanding may result.

Personal development with the Five of Swords card

The Five of Swords represents a time to listen rather than to act or speak. With the disunity caused by the destruction of orthodoxy, the individual may feel empty or like a ship without an anchor. In this situation the key is to wait, watch and learn rather than to attempt to force oneself back into 'normality'. The 'defeat' mentioned in the title of this card occurs when release from the rigidity of conventionality is seen not as a chance for new input but as a fearful state, to be remedied as soon as possible.

THE SIX OF SWORDS

Title:
The Lord of Earned Success
Element: *Air*

In this card the swords are commonly shown in a regular relationship to each other. The overall image is far more balanced and harmonious than any before in this suit.

This card represents the emergence of the Air quality of communication. It shows the development of the human intellect into the procedure known as science. However, this is not the limited mechanical sterility of mind that people often consider to be 'scientific'. As a symbol of communication this image shows the beginnings of union between the intellectual and inspirational qualities of the human psyche.

This is the card of the network, i.e. any system of independent units that are able to interchange information. This applies as much to computer networks as it does to groups of people who exchange ideas and experiences.

Personal development with the Six of Swords card

This card shows the importance of developing a swift communication system to facilitate the exchange of ideas. Psychologically, this is the process of developing an 'inner language' with which the logical and intuitive faculties of the mind can communicate information through all parts of the self. This may be done in any number of ways, one of which is by understanding both the logical and inspirational nature of a system such as the tarot and using it as a means of relating to the workings of both the conscious and unconscious worlds.

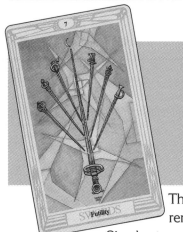

THE SEVEN OF SWORDS

Title:
The Lord of Unstable Effort

Element: *Air*

This card often shows a central sword, reminiscent of the Ace, which is broken. Six shorter weapons seem to be the cause of this breaking up. The holistic feel of the Six has gone, replaced by a less stable image.

The Seven of Swords shows the network structure and communication of the Six having overreached itself and become dissipated. There is unconventionality in this card.

This symbol shows movement in all directions, a whirlwind of activity. However, the direction of enquiry seems to be lost and no definite progress is accomplished. The restlessness and instability of the card shows a lack of trust in the pure process of intellect. At its best, the card show the re-emergence of the emotional forces in the psyche as the partner of the intelligence. At its worst, the card shows the dissipation and dissolution of any definite sense of purpose.

Personal development with the Seven of Swords card

This card warns against overreaching oneself or spreading one's time or abilities too thinly. It is an injunction to use the period that this glyph represents to diversify one's knowledge, to move outside of previously limiting situations.

Again, this card affirms the importance of striking a dynamic harmony between the intellectual and emotional forces in the individual psyche.

THE EIGHT OF SWORDS

Title:
The Lord of Shortened Force

Element: *Air*

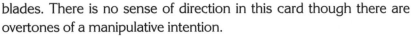

In this card the swords are most characteristically shown pointing in various directions. They may be short or rusted blades. There is no sense of direction in this card though there are overtones of a manipulative intention.

This card shows the Element of Air beginning to re-establish the purpose that was lost in the Seven of Swords. The term 'shortened force' refers to the minor accidents and trials that attend the process of personal development. This could be said to be the card of Murphy's Law!

In this card the manipulative force may be of external circumstances or it may be directed by the individual. In the most productive sense, the Eight of Swords demonstrates the ability to make every incident in life into an occasion for learning and every crisis into an opportunity.

Personal development with the Eight of Swords card

The Eight of Swords shows that the logical process frequently gives rise to more questions than it answers. In trying to discover the mechanism or working of any part of the cosmos the investigative process poses more and more questions. Depending on the mental attitude of the individual, these may represent false starts or problems; alternatively they may be seen as fresh avenues of enquiry.

THE NINE OF SWORDS

Title:
The Lord of Despair and Cruelty

Element: *Air*

This card is most often attended by a fearsome array of symbols. Blood may be seen to drip from the nine downward-pointing swords. Alternatively, the swords may be shown surrounding the figure of a dead man, frequently a knight in armour.

With the exception of Death, the Nine of Swords may be one of the most feared, and misunderstood, images in the tarot.

In this card the Element of Air and the force of Water (as emotionality) begin to align. As they do so, violent forces are released, forces that tear down the old in order to establish a new status quo. The problem arises as this force, like all others, is amoral – this is the card of the Inquisition as much as it is of the inspired religious reformer.

In this card the function of the rational intellect is to analyse, to split apart, that which stands and to slay the outmoded.

Personal development with the Nine of Swords card

The Nine of Swords is very much akin to the Tower of the Major Arcana. It shows the need to cast down the old and prepare the self for new growth. Intellectually, this force may represent a crisis of conscience or of religious or moral ideas. In any case, the 'long dark night of the soul' that this symbol represents occurs swiftly; it is violently carried out but is soon over and done with. The only way out is to take one's medicine and permit this phase to pass.

THE TEN OF SWORDS

Title:
The Lord of Ruin

Element: *Air*

This card often depicts the swords as being fractured and in ruins. Commonly, the ten swords are shown piercing the body of a prostrate human being. In any case, a feeling of sadness and total loss frequently attends this image.

The Ten of Swords is the final card in the suit of Air. It carries with it the emerging ideas that will be developed in the following Earth suit of Discs.

In this card the intellect, belonging to Air, is 'ruined' in the sense that it is seen as being ultimately relativistic. Truth is not a universal absolute; it is dependent on the perception, position and situation of the individual. To give an instance, the 'laws' of Newton apply at the ordinary physical level of everyday phenomena, but in the atomic scale everything is different. Rationality has finally discovered that any law, belief or 'truth' is, in a sense, arbitrary, and that there is no *absolute* reason for anything.

In one sense this card is Ruin because it shows reason divorced from reality, the intellect gone so far off at a tangent as to become completely abstracted from everyday life.

Personal development with the Ten of Swords card

This card counsels against adopting a fanatical or highly abstract mentality and ignoring the relative nature of 'truth'. The Ten of Swords demonstrates the importance of being open to change and the revision of ideas, and even of questioning what appear to be self-evident or absolute truths. It also suggests that the conceptualising process should never be permitted to fly in the face of actual experience – one experimental point of knowledge is worth a thousand idle theorisations.

Ace of Disks

THE ACE OF DISCS

Title:
The Root of the Power of Earth

Element: *Earth*

This card is one on which the designers or publishers of a tarot deck often set their own logo or seal. The central image is of a disc, sometimes with wings or foliage around it. The image is one of completeness and establishment. The harmonious colours of earth are commonly used to reaffirm this meaning.

The Ace of Discs is a single circle or wheel. As such it connects us to the cyclic pattern of the universe. It is the foundation of the earth upon which we live, from which we draw our nourishment, and to which we return when we die. The card represents the order and completeness of the universe. It affirms the sustaining role of the unconscious, which is not at odds with the conscious mind but which supports it and permits it to manifest itself. Symbolically the Ace of Discs is the harmony in the universe and the equality of every Element. Most importantly this card is one of action, of manifestation and of realisation.

Personal development with the Ace of Discs card

This card represents the importance of manifesting inward development of the self at the physical level. It is an injunction to *do,* to seek to be at one with yourself but not to let the work of personal development stop there. Inward understanding must be expressed as much in daily life as in your own unconscious if it is to have any meaning.

The Ace of Discs signifies new growth and an opportunity for the individual to participate fully in the material realm and, by doing so, to discover the harmony of the self expressed outwardly in nature.

THE TWO OF DISCS

Title:
The Lord of Harmonious Change
Element: *Earth*

In this card the two discs are usually depicted as being linked together by a figure of eight. Sometimes this figure is shown as a snake biting its own tail (a very ancient alchemical symbol) or simply as the mathematical symbol for infinity. There is a sense of rotating movement in this card, akin to that of Fortune in the Major Arcana.

In the Two of Discs, the axiom that 'change equals stability' is restated. However, this time the important feature of this idea is shown in the concept of rotation. This symbol shows that all aspects of the universe are most stable when they exist in a rotating form. Thus the ecology of the northern latitudes of the earth remains stable as a whole by fluctuating through a series of stages (seasons), which repeat endlessly. The two discs may be said to represent masculine and feminine, yin and yang, or negative and positive aspects in the human psyche. By rotating, i.e. moving through a progression from one state to another, an integrated whole exists.

Personal development with the Two of Discs card
The Two of Discs represents the stability of all systems (most relevantly the system of the individual psyche) that results from a rotating series of facets within it. It counsels the individual to set out a system of being active then passive, working then playing, waking then sleeping so that a balanced whole person may result. It shows the importance of recognising the seasons, cycles, and shifting aspects that occur in one's life.

THE THREE OF DISCS

Title:
The Lord of Material Works

Element: *Earth*

In this card the discs frequently form the points of a triangle, the first 'closed' or stable figure. This symbolism may be affirmed by showing the discs forming part of a building such as a temple, pyramid or church.

With this card the material or concrete aspect of the Element of Earth comes to the fore. This card is concerned with planning, and with defining one's limits and field of operation. It is the card of construction and work in the sense of being able to apply ideas in actions. This is the card of the engineer; it is the card of structuring and then pursuing one's ambition. In this card, the three discs may be seen as representing the active aspects of Fire, Water and Air which have become mounted or founded upon the Earth force.

Personal development with the Three of Discs card

This card shows the importance of planning and of making certain that one's personal development has a strong foundation. Moreover, this glyph represents the concept that personal development is as much an expression of oneself as it is an internal process. The question posed by this card might well be: 'In what way do you express the truths within yourself?' There is a definite warning against being one way and acting in another. The injunction to get one's hands dirty, to work for one's own individuation and to express it at a concrete level is also included here.

THE FOUR OF DISCS

Title:
The Lord of Earthly Power

Element: *Earth*

This card most commonly shows the work of the Three of Discs as accomplished. The discs may be incorporated into a fortress or castle that sits established in the centre of the scene. The discs become more like keystones or building blocks, firm, though bereft of their rotation shown in the Two.

This is a card of centre. The discs have become interlinked and made solid to form a force of law and order. This symbol represents the created and observable universe in its four dimensions (height, length, breadth and time). The system is stable and tranquil; it does not merely protect what is within it but, like the castles of old, also guards the land that surrounds it.

The Four of Discs is a card of security, permanence, protection and definition, which all living systems require yet which it is impossible to maintain indefinitely.

Personal development with the Four of Discs card

At one level, this card counsels the individual to find security in the self, which will then provide security in dealing with the outside world. On the other hand, the lack of movement exhibited here shows that security is only another point on the endless spiral of change and cannot be clung to forever. This card also demonstrates the importance of finding, in an everyday context, that which will provide a supportive environment for the individual.

THE FIVE OF DISCS

Title:
The Lord of Material Trouble

Element: *Earth*

In this card the scene may be one of poverty or loss. The solid discs of the Four give way to tattered pennies that appear worthless. There is a great sense that the halcyon days of the past are being replaced with bitter troubles.

In this card the stress of maintaining the establishment in the Four of Discs gives way to a breakdown of that system. When people feel certain and secure for any time, the worry that things can only deteriorate generally occurs. In this card, minor changes are shown as occurring, but nothing of lasting value can be accomplished until the stasis of the Four is finally undone.

In one respect, this card represents one of the paradoxes of Earth. While it is the most stable Element, it is also the most dramatically disturbed when it does move. This is the card of the earthquake and of the sudden shattering of the diamond when cut the wrong way.

Personal development with the Five of Discs card

This card shows the necessity of moving outward from the stability of one's centre (the Four) into the uncertain but, potentially, more fruitful realm of experience. The danger in personal development of staying forever centred is that of developing a 'me and God' complex, where the individual is so concerned about preserving an internal stability that outside factors and inner emotions are ignored.

While the attitude that one is secure and focused in oneself appears to be one of inner strength, it actually underlies an inability to reach out and become involved in the universe of experience.

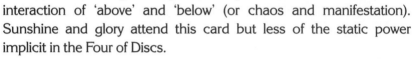

THE SIX OF DISCS

Title:
The Lord of Material Success

Element: *Earth*

In this card the discs resume a more overtly harmonious form. The discs may be shown as forming a hexagram, the symbol of the interaction of 'above' and 'below' (or chaos and manifestation). Sunshine and glory attend this card but less of the static power implicit in the Four of Discs.

In this card the materialisation process, which is the central theme of the Element of Earth, has reached a stable state. This card shows the flowing force of the creative potential both in individual terms and by interaction with others. There is a transience in this symbol which is not to be feared; the uses of the 'change = stability' equation have begun to be applied in a concrete way. On a basic material level, this card could represent the development of a business or other project by dealing with other individuals or agencies.

Personal development with the Six of Discs card

This symbol counsels the individual to look outside the self for sources of inspiration and assistance in the work of individuation. It also shows the importance of using the flux and flow of the seasons (at all levels) to promote one's own purpose. Finally, this card affirms that success is not a full stop but a process and, like any other process, must continually develop and change. Success in the universe exists only to spur the individual on to more questioning.

THE SEVEN OF DISCS

Title:
The Lord of Success Unfulfilled

Element: *Earth*

The addition of a seventh disc unbalances the system of the Six. This card is commonly attended by darkened clouds and organic growth, which has withered through disease or neglect.

There are many differing ways of viewing the symbolism of this card. In one respect this card shows the forces of limitation operating on the expansive energy of the Six of Discs. From another aspect, this card shows neglect and indolence that have been responsible for ruining a promising crop. In a more beneficial sense, while this symbol may represent the death of the flower, this is necessary if the fruit of one's labours is to form. Moreover, outside factors that appear to have only damaging consequences can actually provide new possibilities for growth. A good example of this process is that of biological disease, which may be damaging to the organism but resistant strains eventually build up in the species as a whole.

Personal development with the Seven of Discs card

This card suggests a period when factors that limit or appear harmful to one's purpose may be reconciled and incorporated into one's plans to help rather than hinder. This symbol serves to point out the limitations of the individual which, while theoretically boundless, cannot control everything. Having gained a sense of self-determination through self-development, there may be a tendency to expect everything to submit to one's own designs; this card shows the futility of such an attitude.

THE EIGHT OF DISCS

Title:
The Lord of Prudence
Element: *Earth*

The discs in this card may be represented by flowers upon a regular, well-pruned tree or plant. There is a sense of order but this springs from care taken and not the dominating establishment of the Four.

This is a card of measured, regular and ordered growth. Unlike the more energetic nature of the previous card, the Eight shows a gradual process of study, learning, experience and development. There is a sense of adhering to a carefully arranged plan (much as a vine may be trained around a trellis). The creative energy in this card is conserved. It is not blocked into a limited centre; rather it works through a structured and prudently devised plan.

There is something of retirement and consolidation implicit in this symbol. The creative, manifesting force of Earth is not used to create new systems but instead is used to reaffirm and to consolidate what has gone before.

Personal development with the Eight of Discs card
There are two main messages in this card. The first is that the individual should pursue personal development in an orderly, step-by-step way. By practising and studying regularly, much more may be achieved than by sporadic efforts, however determined. The second message is that a period of revision is necessary. The work of the past does not require analysis, but rather reaffirmation and consolidation to ensure that further work is fruitful.

THE NINE OF DISCS

Title:
The Lord of Material Gain

Element: *Earth*

This card usually shows the discs as coins, arranged in such a manner as to suggest material prosperity. The overall feeling of this card is one of good fortune and gradual but definite growth.

This card continues the motif of organic growth shown in the Eight. The force of Earth becomes increasingly diverse and complex, just as natural systems tend towards diversity and myriad interrelationships. The gain spoken of in the title of this card recalls the exponential growth in any living system. However, gain does not come without hard work and there is a sense of great effort being exerted in this card.

Paradoxically, as the energy of Earth starts to crystallise into more stable, though complex forms, the greater is the degeneration of the original force. This state of entropy may occur at a conscious level; however, the unconscious will always be found brewing a new set of dreams even when it seems all possibilities have been explored.

Personal development with the Nine of Discs card

As a corollary to the 'change = diversity' equation, the Nine of Discs shows that diversity equals strength. It shows that, in the individual psyche, the complexity of elements serves to strengthen the whole. Complexity need not mean complication.

This card counsels the individual to explore the possibilities of applying the understanding of the self in the myriad ways available on the physical level. Finally, it suggests the importance of determined effort to be able to marshal diverse resources in order to perform work of individuation.

THE TEN OF DISCS

Title:
The Lord of Wealth

Element: *Earth*

This is the 'final' card in the whole tarot. It is often shown as being ten discs or coins, the same as the ones the Fool carried in his knapsack at the commencement of the Major Arcana.

The Ten of Discs is a symbol of both manifestation and regeneration. It represents the power of the unconscious, channelled through the conscious mind, manifesting fully at the physical level. The term 'wealth' in the title applies to one's wealth of experience, which is far more valuable than any coinage. It is for this reason that the Fool carries these ten discs for, though he is an innocent figure, he still carries the accrued wealth of his past with him.

There is no definite movement implied in this card. Instead, there is a momentary pause, before stepping once again through the doorway into the 'first' tarot card.

Personal development with the Ten of Discs card

This symbol counsels the individual to review and, most importantly, to value the experience provided by the universe. It shows the importance of manifesting one's nature at all levels – inner and outer, mental and physical. Finally, it represents the process of regeneration and the dawn of new possibilities existing as a seed in every aspect of human experience.

Chapter 7
Continuation

he tarot is a wordless book without beginning or end. This book has a definite end but for you it may herald a new beginning.

The practice of personal development, whatever methods or tools you use, is a continuous procedure. It will change you, and continue to change you. Personal development demands constant revision of your own life – literally 're-vision', to re-see yourself and to assess your position from a new perspective. This book uses the tarot as a tool to accelerate and assist this process.

Having come thus far you may wish to explore other personal development systems – astrology, the I Ching, runes, etc. While the tarot is a valid tool and a complete system, you will benefit by investigating the slightly different approaches that other personal development methods offer. The I Ching and the tarot have much in common, and in fact far more similarities than differences. But by adding more strings to your bow you will have a range of ways to pursue the central aim of self-exploration and individuation.

A vital aspect of personal development, reiterated throughout this text, is the necessity to manifest your own development in an outward form. Your relationships with others will change with the growth of your understanding of your inner nature and your place in the universe as a whole. Personal development is not aloof from daily life but touches every point in your life.

In this book we have examined the tarot using the language of psychology. However, when something is said to be 'psychological' it is often mistakenly seen as being 'unreal' or 'subjective'.

Psychological terminology has its limitations, as does any type of language. This is why the tarot is a picture-book, a collection of images that cannot be adequately described in words. If you have worked through the exercises given in this text you will realise that the tarot has tremendous depth, a rich series of layers of meaning and application. There are many other works on the tarot that may add to your understanding and appreciation of the cards. There will also be events in your own life, yet to come, that will open up new avenues of exploration and provide you with a new perception of the tarot.

Now that you have worked your way through this book, what you have learned will stand you in good stead if you wish to extend your knowledge of the cards, or explore any other personal development system. So this chapter need not be a conclusion but a staging post in a continuous journey, a point upon the revolving wheel of change where each ending is a new beginning.

There is a budding morrow in midnight.

KEATS

Further Reading

Books on the Tarot

Annett, Sally and Shepherd, Rowena, *The Atavist Tarot* (W. Foulsham & Co. Ltd, 2002)

Bridges, Carol, *The Medicine Woman Inner Guidebook* (US Games Systems, 1992)

Crowley, Aleister, *The Book of Thoth* (US Games Systems, 1997)

Eason, Cassandra, *Tarot Talks to the Woman Within* (W. Foulsham & Co. Ltd, 2001)

Kaplan, Stuart R, *The Encyclopedia of Tarot* (US Games Systems, 1990)

Books on Psychology, Myths and Related Subjects

Berne, Eric, *Games People Play* (Penguin, 1968)

Campbell, Joseph, *The Masks of God – Primitive Mythology* (Penguin, 1991)

Jung, CG, *Man and His Symbols* (Picador, 1983)

Neumann, Eric, *The Great Mother* (Princeton University Press, 1992)

Rainwater, Janette, *You're in Charge* (DeVorss & Co., 1985)

Summers, Catherine and Vayne, Julian, *Seeds of Magick* (W. Foulsham & Co. Ltd, 1990)

Books about Other Aspects of Personal Development and Occultism

Butler, Alan, *Personal Development with the Zodiac Oracle* (W. Foulsham & Co. Ltd, 2002)

Crowley, Aleister, *Magick* (Samuel Weiser, 1991)

Eason, Cassandra, *A Practical Guide to Witchcraft and Magick Spells* (W. Foulsham & Co. Ltd, 2000)

Leshan, Lawrence, *How to Meditate* (Little Brown, 1999)

Oken, Alan, *Complete Astrology* (Bantam Books, 1988)

Valiente, Doreen, *Witchcraft for Tomorrow* (Robert Hale, 1993)

Index